Global Warming...Really?

By

Gregory E. Parker

Parker Press

A Book Publishing Company

Global Warming...Really?

Cover designed by Christopher D. Parker
Cover Photo of author By Silver Plate Photography

First Edition 2010
ISBN-10: 0-978801210
ISBN-13: 978-0-978801212

Library of Congress Control Number: 2010900675

Manufactured and bound in the U.S.A

For Jean-Luc, Tasha, Lois, Lashawn,
Christopher, Willie, Eric, Kelly

Contents

Acknowledgements

I am but one working middle-class American with weaknesses and flaws and this book would have been far worse if it were not for the kind help of my friends and colleagues. I am proud to have an opportunity to contribute my thoughts to the world at large. If you are reading this, I hope this book is helpful in your quest for knowledge. I personally want to thank you for taking the time to learn more about global warming.

Thanks to Eric and Kelly Burton for their belief in me, and their friendship, and keeping me grounded. Thanks to Dr. Tim Ball, who after one phone call became an inspiration and friend. Thanks to the citizens of Comal County and the State of Texas for their unwavering support. Thanks to the Media Research Institute for their assistance. Thanks to Kevin Jackson, Joe Bastardi, and David Almasi for their review and being great guys. Thanks to Otto Harrison for the encouragement in a time of trouble and assisting me in moving in the right direction. Thanks to Crosswalk Cafe and Dennis & Jennifer Willson for their assistance. Thanks to Silver Plate Photography for the cover photo of myself.

Greg

Foreword

By

Dr. Tim Ball

The claim that human production of CO_2 is causing global warming and climate change is undoubtedly the biggest deception in history. No previous deception was global or had such massive implications for economies and progress. The fervor with which the deception was promoted created passions that pushed objectivity aside. Large segments of society were bullied into silence while other segments were obliged to publicly express support. If they didn't they were attacked as uncaring about the environment, the children and the future of the planet. It took considerable courage for scientists who understood what was wrong with the science to speak out and many chose to keep quiet. It took even more courage for a politician, even if they had science training. As a result most politicians jumped on the global warming bandwagon especially since there was the potential for massive revenue from carbon taxes. Only a few realized there were problems with the science. Even fewer realized the taxes were unnecessary and potentially harmful to economies and progress.

Many people from various backgrounds have written about global warming providing many perspectives. Almost all the political works have presented the science in a way that underscores lack of understanding of the science. They then pursue the standard political approach of saving the planet by eliminating the threat of global warming. As H.L. Mencken said; "the urge to save humanity is almost always a false face for the urge to rule." It is true the US Senate voted 95 to 0 against signing the Kyoto Accord, but this was because it would cost jobs and harm the economy. They considered this a greater problem than implementing policy based on falsified science.

Gregory has written a book that understands the science or more correctly the bad science. More important he then presents the entire issue from his strength of knowing and understanding the political and economic ramifications of the deception. He recognizes the threat to jobs and economies, but realizes that basing policy on false information is a more profound problem, that meaningful leadership must spring from truth and basic values.

***

Dr. Tim Ball holds a Ph.D. in Climatology and is a renowned environmental consultant and former climatology professor at the University of Winnipeg. Dr. Ball employs his extensive background in climatology and other fields as an advisor to the International Climate Science Coalition, Friends of Science and the Frontier Centre for Public Policy. He has published numerous articles on climate change and its impact on the human condition. Dr. Ball has served on numerous committees on climate, water resources, and environmental issues.

Preface

I decided to write this book after years of witnessing the increasing fervor over the Global Warming debate. As an elected official I have many responsibilities, to my constituents, to my state and to my country. One of those responsibilities is to always seek truth and knowledge even in the face of derision and personal attacks. In an economy that is screaming for assistance and a population hungry for jobs what we really need out of Washington is a real and balanced approach to energy, not additional taxes or more hands reaching into the pockets of hard working Americans. The fact is any comprehensive energy plan must utilize all of the tools in America's energy toolbox, fossil fuels and alternative energy.

America is a unique country that is rich in energy resources. Coal, oil and natural gas reserves buried deep beneath the soil will serve as a source of energy for decades to come but only if we stay committed to a balanced approach to harnessing its potential while at the same time safeguarding the environment which holds this precious commodity. This is a common sense view of reality not the fear based model being peddled by the Global Warming Alarmists and their minions.

This is a critical time in this nation's progression because it is my firm belief that Energy and Energy Technologies will be the next big economy. That is why I wrote this book and that is why I encourage you as a reader and as a citizen to challenge the prevailing wisdom by arming yourself with knowledge. Until recently those who have challenged the conventional wisdom have been left to wander the "Skeptics" world alone. Now it is time to bring everyone to the table to have an honest conversation about where we go from here. As a man of reason I realize that there is in fact merit to both sides of this issue and the solution can always be found somewhere in the middle. It is my hope that this book will help swing the conversation back from the brink of wild ideology, back to a place where reality turns to action that will result in US prosperity.

***

1

Chapter One:
Global Warming...Really?

*"... global warming is in the abolition of private property and production for human need. A socialist world would place an enormous priority on alternative energy sources. This is what ecologically-minded socialists have been exploring for quite some time now." ~ **Louis Proyect***

G lobal warming, what's all the fuss about? This question has been asked of me more than I care to recall. This question, asked by even my mom a diehard democrat, not only started me thinking, but it awakened a now driving hunger to find out knowledge and truth about the global warming issue. Like many of you I have seen Al Gore's "Inconvenient Truth"...... Exaggerations! I like you have been inundated by the endless parade of film documentaries and TV specials focused like a laser on saving the planet and bent on convincing all of us to "go green." I have also, ad nauseum, listened to the political pundits try to "enlighten" me to the fact that there is a complete consensus among scientists that man-made global warming exists and the end of the earth as we know it is near.

I am just your average hardworking adult. Just a guy who grew up to a single mother who worked hard all her life and instilled in us the value of a dollar and that hard work carries the day. I view life from a balanced conservative perspective where if you work hard you can make it. So what follows in these chapters are my opinions based on my research, my experiences and my observations to the issue of global warming. It is my desire that my research, my experiences and my observations can assist the West Virginia coal miner or the single mother from New York; the family of five from Alabama or the newlyweds from Wisconsin to clearly understand the foundation of this issue.

My goal, by writing this book, is not to take the place of your own private exploration into this subject but to become a starting point by which you launch your search for knowledge about what is fast becoming the topic of our time. On with It!

We all know and can see that access to abundant affordable energy is one of the chief reasons we enjoy the wonderful standard of living we have in America. Energy can be counted on to provide power for our homes, fuel for transportation to and from work, and other basic essentials. Yet, a number of under-developed countries do not share in such a similar success. For example, India accounts for 35% of the world's population, yet 33% of India's urban poor and 77% of its rural poor are without electricity connections.[1] While China and East Asia saw an improved economy as they improved access to electricity connections to 99% of their population.[2]

Despite the fact that the economy is the engine of most countries and the United States (US) and energy is the oil that makes that engine run smooth, there is an all-out assault on the very life blood that make the US economy pump. The assault to reduce energy usage in the US has intensified in recent years. Global Warming Alarmist (GWA) claim that fossil fuels such as coal, petroleum, and natural gas are creating too much Carbon Dioxide (CO_2), and the US should remove it immediately; Right Now! Or the world is doomed, to only use renewable energy sources such as bio-fuels, solar, and wind. Nuclear energy according to global warming alarmist can't save us because it is too polluting, too dangerous, too expensive, and unnecessary.[3]

So let's get some clear facts. According to the US Energy Information Administration Annual Energy Review Report, 84% of the energy consumed in the United States comes from fossil fuels, petroleum, coal and natural gas, with crude oil-based petroleum products as the dominant source of energy.[4]

Renewable energy resources supply a minimal 7% of U.S. total energy consumption and nuclear fuel generates only 9% of the US energy consumption.[5] Yet there are recent reports that renewable energy has overtaken nuclear again.[6]

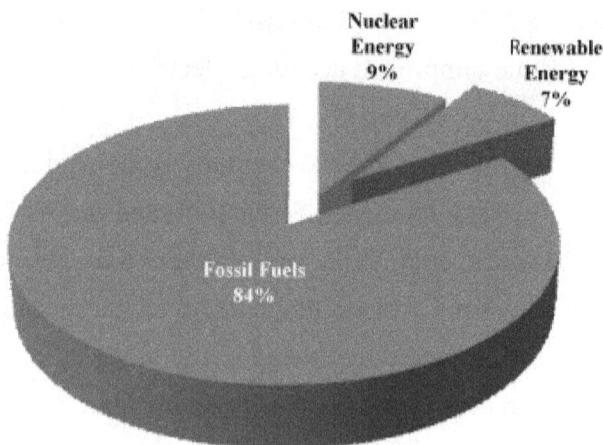

With that said most Americans still appear to be motivated much more by finances than by environmental concerns. This is never more clear then when it comes to making their homes more energy efficient. According to a recent Gallup/USA Today poll 71% of Americans who have taken steps to make their homes more energy efficient say they did so to save money rather than to improve the environment.[7] I'm sure you can guess there was a distinct division along ideology as it relates to cost savings versus the environment. GWA were more likely to give the environment a greater priority and conservatives far less likely to, but a majority of GWA still citing cost savings as their primary reason for taking those actions.[8]

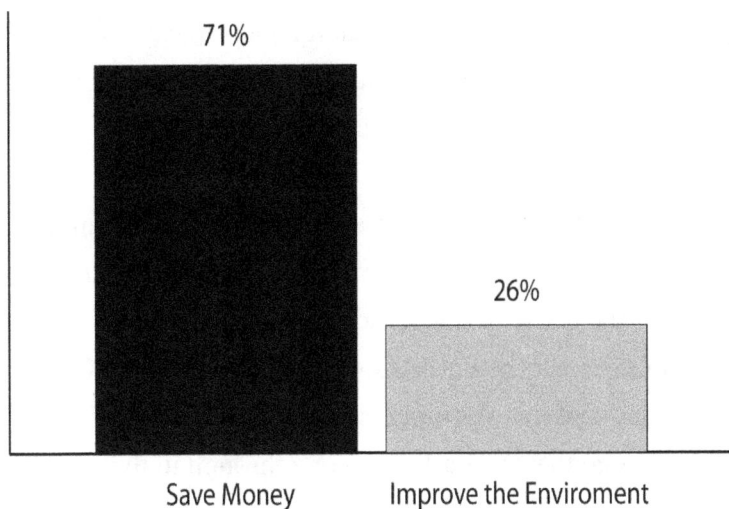

71%

26%

Save Money   Improve the Enviroment

USA Today/Gallup Poll

This greater emphasis on economics may not necessarily be the case under normal economic circumstances. For the first time, more Americans said economic growth ought to be a higher priority than protecting the environment.[2] This maybe why the 2009 "cap-n-trade" bill has stalled in the U.S. Senate, but we will talk about that later.

With that said I think it would be wise for me to define the term "Global Warming." I also believe it is important to note I will be using global warming and climate change somewhat interchangeably thought-out this book.

When you say global warming around some conservatives an audible moan and sometimes a loud snicker can clearly be heard. A lot of misconception exists around this term. Newt Gingrich himself said that "…for too many years, liberals have defined what it means to care about the environment -- and too often at a level that is so radical, so hysterical and so inaccurate that the first reaction of conservatives is to oppose them."[10]

The National Oceanic and Atmospheric Administration (NOAA) defined global warming, without any implications for the cause or magnitude, as the observation that the atmosphere near the Earth's surface is warming.[11] NOAA also noted that this warming is one of many kinds of climate change that the Earth has gone through in the past and will continue to go through in the future.[12]

I personally believe we have allowed GWAs to dominate and hold the high ground on this issue.[13] GWAs use ill-conceived policies that focus on wealth redistribution and legal action instead of science, instead of free markets solutions and incentives. Well, no more!

There is a place for those of us who are not GWAs, those of us who want our lawmakers to finally create and implement a long-term energy plan that will balance supply and demand, and ensure reliable and affordable supplies of energy for our children's future.[14] Those of us who believe the real goal should be to balance and blend the responsible utilization of all energy resources while maintaining a strong vibrant economy and protecting private property rights, not protecting ideology.

We need not look at global warming through the GWA lens stained by lies and fraud. Because it is a fact the Earth's climate changes from day to day, in the simplest

GREGORY E. PARKER

of terms it's called "weather." We disagree with GWAs as to the level in which man is the underlining cause of such climate change.

Global warming is not bad; the GWA's radicalization and lies about global warming is bad.

Is CO_2 Causing It?

Science has revealed that the earth's average temperature has increased during the past century, some of the highest temperatures occurred in 1876, 1897, 1892, 1890, and 1891 well before human emissions could have been responsible for global warming.[15] These increases have been well within levels most humans will not even notice. But with those facts alone GWAs have sold the populous that the world will end soon.

It is a common GWA belief that CO_2 levels precede higher temperature levels. This is at the core of their argument that humans are at the center of creating large amounts of CO_2 gases which drive up the earth's temperature. This is proving to be incorrect. Data for any time period in the history will show any CO_2 increase were always preceded by temperature increases.[16] This would mean the UN's International Panel on Climate Change (IPCC) computer models themselves are completely inadequate to represent global climate or make any predictions about future climate. For the most part, predicting climate change using computer models have been proven to be inaccurate at best.[17] Author and environmental activist Guy Dauncey admitted as much in his book The Climate Challenge.[18] It is also in the IPCC's own Technical Report ("The Physical Science Basis") released in November 2007.[19] Further, the IPCC own report cast doubts on the science and the claim that the Southern Ocean is reaching its saturation point:

"Systematic biases have been found in most models simulation of the Southern Ocean. Since the Southern Ocean is important for ocean heat uptake, this results in some uncertainty in transient climate response." ~The Physical Science Basis Report – IPCC - November 2007

This is important because the earth's oceans create CO_2 and play a key role in regulating and or mitigating the amount of CO_2 in the atmosphere since oceans cover 70% of the earth's surface.[20]

Wolfgang Knorr from the University of Bristol published a study which noted that the fraction of human emitted CO_2 that remains in the atmosphere has generally stayed constant over the past 160 years, at least within the limits of measurement uncertainty.[21]

"Several recent studies have highlighted the possibility that the oceans and terrestrial ecosystems have started losing part of their ability to sequester a large proportion of the

*anthropogenic CO_2 emissions. This is an important claim, because so far only about 40% of those emissions have stayed in the atmosphere, which has prevented additional climate change. This study re-examines the available atmospheric CO_2 and emissions data including their uncertainties. It is shown that with those uncertainties, the trend in the airborne fraction since 1850 has been 0.7 ± 1.4% per decade, i.e. close to and not significantly different from zero. The analysis further shows that the statistical model of a constant airborne fraction agrees best with the available data if emissions from land use change are scaled down to 82% or less of their original estimates. Despite the predictions of coupled climate-carbon cycle models, no trend in the airborne fraction can be found." ~ **Wolfgang Knorr- University of Bristol**

Atmospheric CO_2 measurements date back quite a while. Scientists took readings with instruments, as the work of Ernst-Georg Beck has thoroughly documented.[22] Guy Stewart Callendar's data, for which most of the International Panel of Climate Change (IPCC) reports are based, rejects most of the early data electing to use only 69% of the 19th century climate records. His clear omissions of data established a pre-industrial CO_2 levels at 280 ppm for the IPCC reports.[23]

Ernst-Georg Beck article 180 Years of Atmospheric CO_2 Gas Analysis by Chemical Methods examined the readings in great detail and validated the historical measurements indicated fluctuating CO_2 levels between 300 and more than 400 ppmv once you take into account non-omitted data.[24] Beck explains:

> *"Modern greenhouse hypothesis is based on the work of G.S. Callendar and C.D. Keeling, following S. Arrhenius, as latterly popularized by the IPCC. Review of available literature raises the question if these authors have systematically discarded a large number of valid technical papers and older atmospheric CO_2 determinations because they did not fit their hypothesis?"[25]*

Furthermore, according to the 2008 report, U.S. Energy Information Administration's Emissions of Greenhouse Gases in the United States, CO_2 emissions have gone down 14% since 1990 and down 0.7% in 2007.[26] Yet we have widely heard 2009 was the 5th hottest year on record.[27] Really.....? CO_2 levels down while temperatures went up, Hmmm!

New emerging climate science from the National Aeronautics and Space Administration (NASA) based on observational satellite measurements of climate variables in the upper atmosphere showed that after five years of NASA data we can clearly see minimal to no impact on temperatures from man-made CO_2.[28]

That emerging science has produced a study from NASA's Goddard Space Flight Center in Greenbelt, Maryland looking at climate data over the past century. That report found that solar variation made a significant impact on the Earth's climate.[29]

Really? *"Because it is those pushing this silly theory that our puny SUVs and power plants are causing earth to warm up when the most obvious source of heat hangs over their head every single day."*[30]

Could it be that maybe the sun has more to do with global warming than man? Hmmm?

Greenhouse Effect and Global Warming?

The earth's atmospheric properties are very simple to understand. The National Oceanic and Atmospheric Administration (NOAA) Office of Oceanic and Atmospheric Research (OAR) explained the earth's atmosphere is made up of 78% Nitrogen, 21% Oxygen, and 1% trace gases.[31] Those trace gases, also called "greenhouse gases", are a mixture of water vapor, carbon dioxide (CO_2) and other.[32] These greenhouse gases create what is commonly called the "greenhouse effect" which allows energy from the sun to reach the earth's surface, but absorb emitted energy from the earth; this affects the surface energy balance of the planet by warming the atmosphere directly above it.[33]

The term "greenhouse effect" is somewhat misleading because the earth's atmosphere does not truly work like an actual greenhouse. An actual greenhouse would have a roof of glass that traps the radiation emitted from the ground and operate as a barrier to convection (the rising of hot air). While the atmosphere really facilitates convection, based on certain molecules, absorbing radiation and reemitting a portion back to the ground.[34] This creates the impression of actual greenhouse-like activity in the Earth's atmosphere.[35]

According to the NOAA, some greenhouse gases occur naturally: Water vapor, Carbon dioxide (CO_2), Methane (CH4), Nitrous oxide (N2O), and others are man-made industrial gases: Hydrofluorocarbons (HFCs), Perfluorocarbons (PFCs), and Sulfur hexafluoride (SF6).[36]

Contrary to the hype around CO_2, water vapor is the most abundant greenhouse gas in the atmosphere and yet the least measured.[37] Water vapor is 95% of the greenhouse gases by volume and CO_2 is less than 4%, but somehow water vapor is virtually ignored.[38]

"...while we have good atmospheric measurements of other key greenhouse gases such as carbon dioxide and methane, we have poor measurements of global water vapor..." ~ **National Oceanic and Atmospheric Administration.**

After reading this statement by the NOAA I was troubled. They have very poor measurements of global water vapor, did I read that right? "…we have poor measurements of global water vapor…" Yep, I read that right, the one greenhouse gas that is most evident. Really… I wonder if global warming is caused by water vapor and not CO_2? Hmmm! But I digress, the "greenhouse effect" is the how, global warming is the how much.

Polar Bears Losing Their Homes, Really?

This question comes up most often in the global warming debate and is considered by GWA to be a large piece of the evidence in their argument for global warming. For years environmentalists and GWA have claimed that the polar bears are gradually going extinct, due to global warming and the melting of the polar ice caps. Well Mitchell Taylor, a polar bear expert with more than 30 years of study and research management into the animals around the Canadian arctic cycle, was banned from the International Union for the Conservation of Nature/Species Survival Commission meeting in June 2009. This meeting was to produce a report on the polar bear counts in a run up to the Copenhagen Climate Conference in December 2009.[39]

Dr. Taylor disagrees that rising levels of CO_2, as is dictated by the UN's Intergovernmental Panel on Climate Change (IPCC) are the reason for global warming. He believes it is due to sea currents bringing warm water into the Arctic from the Pacific.[40]

Dr Taylor's research noted that the polar bear population is much higher than it was 30 years ago. Of the 19 different bear populations in the arctic, most are increasing or at optimum levels, only two have for local reasons modestly declined.[41] The polar bears have gone from 5,000 in 1950 to an estimated 25,000 currently.[42]

As for the ice caps, John Christy the director of the Earth System Science Center at University of Alabama-Huntsville acknowledged a true fact in an interview with Fortune magazine, "Ice melts. Glaciers are always calving. This is what ice does. If ice did not melt, we'd have an ice-covered planet." He also noted that ice cover is growing in the southern hemisphere even as the ice cover is more or less shrinking in the northern hemisphere.[43]

"As you and I are talking today, global sea ice coverage is about 400,000 square kilometers above the long-term average - which means that the surplus in the Antarctic is greater than the deficit in the Arctic." ~ **John Christy**

Additionally, British geographers have now discovered a group of previously uncharted glaciers. The new glaciers, the largest of which is the size of six football pitches, were discovered in the Prokletije Mountains which extends from Northern Albania and Kosovo to Eastern Montenegro in the Western Balkans.[44]

Scientific Consensus?

The Media and GWA have been screaming for ten years or more that there is a scientific consensus that global warming is real and on that fact alone the debate is over. Americans do not see it that way, according to a Rasmussen survey 52% of Americans believe there continues to be significant disagreement within the scientific community over global warming, while just 25% of Americans think most scientists agree on the topic and 23% are not sure.[45]

The IPCC process and reports, given they are produced by the "United Nations" was according to itself to be reflective of a consensus of the scientific community. According to the Merriam-Webster Online Dictionary, consensus is defined as a general agreement; the consensus of their opinion; group solidarity in sentiment and belief.[46] A group of scientists drafted the IPCC report and they are in agreement! With that said, based on that common definition it appears a consensus does exist that global warming is real and man is the underlying cause. Wait! Let us not forget that based on that same common definition consensus also exist that global warming is hype and man is not the major cause.

In 2008, 32,000 scientists signed a petition dissenting from the alarmist assertions of Al Gore and the United Nations Intergovernmental Panel on Climate Change (IPCC).[47] In addition, on March 16, 2009 more than 700 international scientists, 52 of which have authored IPCC reports in the past, have dissented over man-made global warming claims, debunking the notion of a one-sided consensus.[48]

Further, in 2009 in an Open Letter to German Chancellor Angela Merkel, more than 60 prominent German scientists publicly declared their dissent from man-made global warming. This letter apparently includes several United Nations IPCC scientists.[49]

Not only that but, John Christy the director of the Earth System Science Center at University of Alabama-Huntsville, a veteran climatologist and lead author of the 2001 Intergovernmental Panel on Climate Change report as well as one of the three authors of the American Geophysical Union's landmark 2003 statement on climate change, also believes that global warming fears are overblown. Scientific consensus, Really?

***

2
Chapter Two:
Leaders for the Cause, Really?

*"Example is not the main thing in influencing others, it is the only thing."~ **Albert Schweitzer***

Lawrence Meyers, an author on the Blogger News Network, recounted an argument he had with a Global Warming Alarmist (GWA) friend of his and it went something like this.

Friend: Global warming will cause the extinction of mankind within our lifetime unless we do something about it.

Meyers: Wow! That sounds serious, what are you doing about it?"

Friend: I recycle and I carpool.

Meyers: Wait a second. That's it? The Apocalypse is upon us and all you do is recycle cans, and carpool?[1]

These wild outlandish claims have come to symbolize the GWA movement with little regard for the consequences or thought as to how ridiculous they sound.

"I propose a limitation be put on how many squares of toilet paper can be used in any one sitting, ...easy ways for us all to become a part of the solution to global warming," ~ **Sheryl Crow**

"...the grim reality is that our planet has reached a point of crisis and we have only seven years before we lose the levers of control... This, I fear, is not an overstatement." ~ **Prince Charles 2009 UN Copenhagen Climate Change Summit.**[2]

"These figures are fresh. Some of the models suggest...that there is a 75 per cent chance that the entire north polar ice cap, during the summer months, could be completely ice-free within five to seven years." **~ Al Gore 2009 UN Copenhagen Climate Change Summit.**

Leadership according to the Merriam-Webster Dictionary is 1) the office or position of a leader, or 2) capacity to lead, or 3) the act or an instance of leading.[3]

Researchers in the field of leadership as well as most Americans would agree that leadership is more than just an office or the capacity to lead. Leadership is the ability to inspire, and is just as much about the ones being led as it is the leader.

The reality is that any person can lead, yet the ones being led need at least a basic desire to do what is being required of them. The fundamental desire that should be held by those being led is called "credibility," the quality or power, of inspiring belief.[4] This is one of the core abilities that leaders need to inspire belief in those they lead. A fervent belief that the leader is capable of leading and that the leader can at any time do the same job the follower is asked to do.

Let's be real, this is why we would not promote a general to lead troops who has not first been a soldier, or why we would not take parenting advice from someone that doesn't have kids. No Credibility!

Those being led have a keen desire to know that the person leading them is also following the same advice they are espousing. If the leader is not we call that hypocrisy, and we have a saying for that, "Do as I say, not as I do."

That brings me to Lawrence's friend. If he truly believed the earth was in danger and started making these wild apocalyptic claims then he would want to do a lot more than just recycle and park his car. He would become Amish and live "off the grid," or buy solar panels and other alternative energy sources for his home. If you really, truly and firmly believe in something it would radiate out of you no matter what the position, time or place.

GWAs have an overwhelming desire to have others sacrifice their life style, their economy, yet they do little to show any greater level of commitment themselves. It is clear that lack of commitment on their part hurts the credibility of their cause. If they really want to lead their cause, their actions should match their words! Otherwise no one will follow!

As an elected official myself, I have often said over and over again that politicians are either arrogant or stupid; they are that arrogant to think that we are that stupid that we won't notice their hypocrisy. There is a difference between elected officials, who work with and for the people that elected them and politicians who care little for the input of the citizenry and covet the power of the office more than serving the will of the people. The town hall meetings across the country in August 2009 and the healthcare legislation of 2009 – 2010 shined a large light on which leaders were there for themselves and which leaders were there for their constituents.

It is also my experience that political leaders can best shape the opinions of their constituents by displaying the way forward rather than just telling them about it. If constituents can see that their elected leaders are committed to a cause by living that cause they are more likely to follow that example.

Alexandria, VA., a leading GWA movement member travels with eleven large Chevy SUVs, none of them had any signs identifying them as hybrid vehicles, plus an ambulance idling close by. Peter Roff, in his account of a visit he made to an ice cream shop, wondered why the GWAs were not angered by this clear lack of concern for the atmosphere and or the carbon footprint left behind by one of their beloved leaders. What example is this leader displaying for the rest of us? Who is the leader in question? **President Obama**. Now I understand that safety is a concern for the President, but if he really believed in his cause he could use hybrid vehicles or down size to bullet-proof smart cars.[5]

A huge Nashville, Tennessee 10,000-square-foot, 20-room mansion consumes over 20 times the electricity of an average American home. According to the Tennessee Center for Policy Research, it consumes twice as much power in the month of August 2006 than most American homes do in an entire year. The owner spends $500 a month just to heat the indoor swimming pool.[6] What example is this leader displaying for the rest of us? Who was the leader? **Al Gore**. Gore gave the usual response when he was caught not practicing what he preaches. He said he made up for his consumption of electricity and production of carbon dioxide by buying carbon offsets.[7]

Washington D.C. a House Select Committee on Energy Independence in June 2007, the leader of one of the largest cities in America told congressional leaders that his city is leading by example on the global warming issues. He claimed the city was reducing greenhouse gas emissions yet, a recent article in that cities tribune newspaper, affirmed the city's greenhouse gas emissions had actually risen 10% since 2001 and the city is using 22% more electricity than it did in 2003.[8] Who is the leader? **Mayor Richard M. Daley**. What example is this leader displaying for the rest of us?

Massachusetts, just eight miles from this great global warming evangelist home, Jim Gordon, a wind farm developer seeks to use wind power to replace the state's electric power plants. To Jim Gordon's disbelief the proposed wind farm project draws opposition in this state of liberal activist.[9] It was revealed later that this leader had a role in secret behind-the-scenes maneuvering to stop the proposed wind farm project.[10] What example is this leader displaying for the rest of us? What leader would try to undermine the very cause they claim to believe in so strongly? **Former Sen. Ted Kennedy!** Even some Environmental groups launched aggressive campaigns to persuade other Democrats to abandon Kennedy and back the renewable energy project.[11]

The United Nations (UN) Intergovernmental Panel on Climate Change (IPCC) claims to be the leading body for the assessment of climate change and whose mission is "to provide the world with a clear scientific view on the current state of climate change as well as its environmental and socio-economic consequences."[12] With that said I would expect the leaders in this organization to truly believe in their cause. Maybe not?

Dr Rajendra Pachauri: The IPCC chairman himself flew more than 400,000 miles on IPCC business in a 19 month period. That included trips for such things as honorary degree ceremonies and book launch dinners, the latter involving a flight of 3500 miles.[13] He generated 100 tons of CO_2 which he claims to have mitigated by giving J.P. Morgan around $1450 to make his travels carbon-neutral. I will say this again later, but "the earth does not take cash." Paying for forgiveness does not negate the fact that he still released the CO_2 into the air.[14]

Further, the IPCC chairman is now embattled in conflict-of-interest charges in his home country of India. Apparently his close association to The Energy Research Institute (TERI), India's Oil and Natural Gas Commission (ONGC), Indian Oil Corporation (IOC) and National Thermal Power Corporation (NTPC), three of India's biggest public sector energy companies, and other carbon trading companies, have amassed him a fortune.[15] These focal fuel companies and a research firm now appear to be heavily invested in every kind of renewable or sustainable technology.[16] Hmmm?

World Leader and US Congress: The United Nations sponsored a summit on climate change in Copenhagen, Denmark in December 2009 where some 15,000 delegates and officials, 5,000 journalists and 98 world leaders, 140 extra private jets and 1,200 limos were in attendance. The eleven-day conference, including the participant's travel will create 41,000 tons of CO_2 which is equal to the amount produced by a small US city for the same time period.[17]

The US delegation for this Copenhagen trip totaled an estimated 101 people, including staff, spouses, children, and needed three military jets to transport them all. The estimated cost of the flights alone ran the US tax payers $168,000 and released enough CO_2 into the air to fill 10,000 Olympic swimming pools.[18] I don't think these world leaders have ever heard of video conferencing. It would reduce the CO_2 emissions they claim are bringing about the world's end and save the US tax payers some money. Further it would restore some level of credibility to this issue.

Environmental activists and others have a long and some would say proud history of fighting for the GWA causes. I believe their actions do more of a real harm to their cause than helping it.

William Connolley: The Cambridge-based scientist and Green Party activist has single handedly created or re-written more than 5,428 unique climate Wikipedia articles.

"His control over Wikipedia was greater still, however, through the role he obtained at Wikipedia as a website administrator,

*which allowed him to act with virtual impunity. When Connolley didn't like the subject of a certain article, he removed it — more than 500 articles of various descriptions disappeared at his hand. When he disapproved of the arguments that others were making, he often had them barred — over 2,000 Wikipedia contributors who ran afoul of him found themselves blocked from making further contributions. Acolytes whose writing conformed to Connolley's global warming views, in contrast, were rewarded with Wikipedia's blessings. In these ways, Connolley turned Wikipedia into the missionary wing of the global warming movement."~ **Lawrence Solomon***

Connolley was successful in rewriting the Medieval Warm Period, causing the supposedly neutral Wikipedia to provide disclaimers on these and other pages. The release of the Climategate emails has exposed Connolley deceit and manipulation of the truth to fit the GWA agenda.[19] I would argue there is no need to rewrite anything if your science is sound. Further what example does this set for those who may be in search for knowledge about this issue?

Anne Sholtz, was the co-created of the Regional Clean Air Incentives Market (RECLAIM) in California. In 2005, Sholtz plead guilty to wire fraud for using counterfeit credits, from a company Sholtz created to provide a market for companies to buy and sell pollution credits under RECLAIM, pocketing more than $12 million.[20]

Maurice Strong: The founding director of the U.N. Environment Programe (UNEP), a division of the U.N. left his post at the UNEP in the 1970s but kept his ecological credentials is now on leave from the U.N. while questions concerning a $1 million check given to him by South Korean businessman Tongsun Park, who was convicted in Federal Court of conspiring to bribe U.N. officials.[21]

John Travolta: who owns and flies five private planes, claimed the solution to global warming could be found in outer space and blamed his hefty flying mileage on the nature of the movie business. "I'm probably not the best candidate to ask about global warming because I fly jets. I use them as a business tool though, as others do. I think its part of this industry – otherwise I couldn't be here doing this and I wouldn't be here now."[22]

There are so many more examples, yet time and or space will not permit me from listing them all. After reading all these clear examples of do as I say and not as I do, you would assume this would convince GWA supporters their leaders clearly do not believe in the cause. On the contrary GWA supporters argue the actions of their political, scientific, and movie idols ability to steal money, manipulate and destroy data and dump tons of CO_2 in the atmosphere by offering this explanation, "…the person ought to be distinguished from the credibility of a proposition," one blogger wrote.[23] Really!

This is laughable. This is not a Republican or

Democrat thing this is a right and wrong thing. GWA leaders are not inspiring a belief in their cause because it is all too clear they themselves do not believe. If they did they would prove those beliefs in their actions regardless of the place the time or the position. Why should we heed their outlandish cries to utilize less energy or impose on ourselves economy ending environmental schemes of which they exempt themselves?

Let me be clear I am not criticizing these individuals for their ability to make lots money, take trips to foreign countries or live the "American" dream, however, I do criticize their need to steal or destroy others dreams of prosperity under the guise of global warming, climate change or an un-balanced energy policy.

***

3 Chapter Three: There's Money in It, Really?

*"Focusing your life solely on making a buck shows a poverty of ambition. It asks too little of yourself. And it will leave you unfulfilled."~ **Pres. Barack Obama***

The global warming community was rocked by the release of some very damaging emails known around the world as "ClimateGate." According to an article in the Wall Street Journal, the world's leading climate scientists, from the University of East Anglia's Climate Research Unit (CRU), have conspired to block freedom of information requests, black list dissenting scientists, influence the peer-review process, and destroy and manipulate climate research data. All in an effort to make global warming appear more severe. I believe it is interesting to note that the CRU's climate data was one of the primary sources of data for the Intergovernmental Panel on Climate Change (IPCC) 2007 global warming climate change reports.[1] The report was hailed by most governments and cited by the IPCC as the definitive consensus regarding climate science.

To make things worse, Andrei Illarionov, a former economic adviser to then-Russian President Putin and head of his own think-tank, stated that the CRU's dataset doesn't include records from many of Russia's meteorological stations. He further noted that those missing records would have significantly reduced the amount of warming shown for Russia in the CRU database.[2] The CRU's response:

"The World Meteorological Organization chooses the set of stations designated as essential climate stations that have been released by the Met Office. ...We do not choose these stations and therefore it is impossible for the Met Office to fix the data."[3]

Hmmm, another organization connected with the IPCC chooses the climate stations -- I don't know about you but that sounds a lot like stacking the deck and passing the buck to me.

Speaking of buck, the major question I keep asking myself is what would make these scientists cherry-pick, manipulate and destroy climate data given their so called claim that climate change science is "settled."

We know the need for money, power and prestige is a desire of every human, so let's not kid ourselves, scientists are only human. Keep the apocalyptic climate predictions flowing, you keep the money flowing. Really!

Richard S. Linszen, a Massachusetts Institute of Technology professor, noted in his paper Climate Science: Is it currently designed to answer questions, that scientists have switched to fear as a means of support. That fear has several advantages over the gratitude of the community.[4] He recognized that gratitude was limited by the capacity of the community and is less effective, while fear motivates greater generosity from the fearful, to find and fix what is scaring them.[5]

This new shift for scientists into a dependence on a fear based support system is particularly vulnerable to corruption because scientists focus on perpetuating the problem to gather funding, rather than theory and observation.[6] For this end research institutions and schools have created more staff and funding centers just to gather funding. Some tenured professors are evaluated based on the amount of funding their research can gather for the school.[7]

Let's consider just how much money is at stake here. Phil Jones, the man at the heart of "ClimateGate" in one of the emails admits that between 2000 and 2006 Mr. Jones was the recipient (or co-recipient) of some $19 million worth of research grants, a six-fold increase over his grant awards in the 1990s.

GREGORY E. PARKER

*"Billions of dollars of grant money is flowing into the pockets of those on the man-made global warming bandwagon... Nothing wrong with making money at all. But when money becomes the motivation for a scientific conclusion, then we have a problem."~ **James Spann**

June 2009 controversial "Climategate" and Penn State professor Michael Mann, inventor of the now de-bunked "hockey stick" graph of temperature changes over 1000 years, received $541,184 grant from stimulus funds. Several critics of Professor Mann's research call on Penn State to return the money citing the Professor's link to climate data manipulation and the fact that his research does not create jobs as the stimulus was intended to do.[8]

Boise State University increased its external research and grant awards by 77% in 2009. The university recorded its highest quarterly total in school history with $16.1 million up from $9.1 million in external grant awards for the first quarter of fiscal year 2010.[9]

The University of Wyoming recorded receiving a record $81 million in external funding in the 2008-09 fiscal year. $586,581 was allocated to the Department of Atmospheric Science for research on various aspects of climate change and $149,961 used to study how the timing of summer precipitation affects responses of boreal forest to changes in the climate.[10]

Obtaining funding for research is not at all improper, but perpetuating the problem by manipulating the research to fit the problem to gather funding is wrong.

The European Commission most recently appropriated nearly $3 billion, not including funding from the member governments for climate research.[11] In addition by the EU's own calculations it estimates it will spend €60 billion annually on renewable energy projects.[12]

The U.S. intends to allocate $1.3 billion to NASA's climate research, $400 million to NOAA's, and another $300 million to the National Science Foundation, all for climate efforts. Let's not forget the state that is bankrupt, California allocated more than $600 million to their own climate initiatives.[13] Where has all the money gone?

Barack Obama negotiated a non-binding agreement at the UN's December 2009 Copenhagen Climate Summit, to include a $30 billion dollar "quick-start" aid from 2010-2012, and an additional $100 billion a year from 2012 - 2020 all for developing countries which include China.[14]

So let me get this straight, we are going to borrow money from China just to give it back as a gift, without paying the debt we owe. President Obama is not the only President to lay out the funding for climate change. The Bush administration also allocated $20 billion to the "green" cause.[15]

GWAs in Australia have their own Climate Change Department with full government funding at their disposal.

All of this is just a portion of the $94 billion HSBC Bank estimates it will spend globally just this year on what it calls "green stimulus" alternative energy schemes.[16] Wow!

Al Gore, the king of the global warming alarmist movement, wins the Nobel Peace Prize in 2007 and since leaving the Vice-Presidents office in 2001 his estimated net worth has jumped to over $100 million from just over $2 million.[17]

Let us not forget Cap and Trade. Several definitions exist, but cap and trade in the simplest of terms is a government imposed cap on carbon or greenhouse gas emissions (cap), and a government created market to buy and sell those carbon or greenhouse gas emission credits (trade). Notice government is mentioned most in that definition, but I digress.

According to the New York Times, the carbon trading market is currently worth well over $30 billion and is proving to be one of the fastest-growing specialties in the financial services industry and it is expected to grow to $1 trillion within a decade.[18] The Congressional Budget Office estimates the cap and trade market to have a value estimated at $50 billion to $300 billion annually.[19]

Any carbon trading system after it is setup is enormously susceptible to massive fraud. Come on, you didn't think only the "good" guys were going to make all the money. According to the Europol police agency the European carbon trading system has fallen victim to organized crime during the past 18 months of operation. They stated the criminal activity is believed to have resulted in system losses of roughly $7.4 billion. The Europol police agency estimates that in some countries as much as 90 percent of the entire market volume of the carbon trading system was fraudulent activities.

"This is the problem with politicians trying to create a market for something that the free market otherwise doesn't value..." ~ **Max Schulz, Senior Fellow at the Manhattan Institute.**

Europol officials explained the scam:
Traders would open accounts in a carbon registry and then purchase emission allowances without value added taxes from other companies in other countries. Those allowances were then transferred to the country where they were registered before the traders moves them to an unregulated broker, selling the allowances on a trading exchange, often through various buffer companies. Finally, the accused trader charges the value added tax on the transaction but does not submit that money to authorities.[20]

Do these cap and trade or carbon trading systems actually work? According to Open Europe's report "Europe's Dirty Secret: Why the EU Emissions Trading Scheme Isn't Working," emissions in the UK from

2005-2006 actually rose 3.6% and for countries covered by the EU's cap and trade system emissions rose overall by 0.8%.[21] The report, perhaps foreseeing 2009's Europol police agency findings, noted that the EU system has established a web of politically powerful interest groups, massive economic distortions, covert industrial subsidies and it will do practically nothing to fight climate change.[22]

Opponents of the European model of carbon trading system warn this will be happing in the US if we implement this style of cap-and-trade system. Further according to Staffing and the Greenhouse Gas Management Institute the world's carbon trading markets are extremely vulnerable to accounting scandals like those of Enron, WorldCom and Tyco.[23].

Speaking of Enron, the failed energy company pushed hard for cap-and-trade during its existence. Enron believed cap-and-trade would allow them to dominate the US energy market by requiring electric utilities to switch from coal to natural gas or carbon offsets, of which Enron was already a major player.[24]

With these failures why would politicians engage in such reckless policies? In an op-ed in the Roanoke Times Paul J. Georgia said it best:

> *"...Because cap-and-trade is a complex regulatory scheme that hides the true costs of compliance from taxpayers. Politicians can regulate energy use through the hidden*

Really?

tax of cap-and-trade to avoid accountability, creating the perfect cover for vultures like Enron to swoop in and capture the rewards." ~ **Paul J. Georgia**

Yet I am convinced the earth doesn't take cash or visa. You can't buy forgiveness and it is a mistake to believe you can.

With all this money up for grabs, it's clear by keeping the apocalyptic climate predictions coming; you keep the money coming, whether you are an organization or an individual within the GWA movement. It is also clear that the direction of research has quickly become predetermined given most applicants have learned to add appropriate keywords the funding agencies want in their grant applications.

Now let me be perfectly clear, I am for free market solutions. I believe companies and individuals making money is not a bad thing. I just want for myself and the American people truth in advertising. If you're going to sell me or the citizenry on the global warming product, then tell me the truth about what we're buying.

It is not necessary for GWAs and their leaders to bash and trash corporations and their profits in an effort to push an ideology, when they are doing the exact same thing under the guise of "protecting" the earth.

***

4

Chapter Four:
Green Jobs, Really?

"...My presidency will mark a new chapter in America's leadership on climate change that will strengthen our security and create millions of new jobs in the process." - **President-elect Barack Obama, Global Climate Summit, November 18, 2008**

On January 8, 2010 to the clamor of press and photographers alike, President Obama announces that $2.3 billion in federal tax credits will be issued to create 17,000 new "green" jobs.[1] After watching the press conference I found myself asking two obvious questions, what is a "green" job and how can we truly measure "green" job success if the definition of those jobs could best be described as vague?

Advocates argue these jobs will ease unemployment, help reduce climate change and the nation's dependence on foreign oil. While opponents question the very sustainability of such "green" jobs and whether the government has the ability to even identify such jobs.

What is a "green" job?

At present there is no clear definition of "green" jobs, as a matter a fact several broad definitions exist. So it should come as no surprise that there is even debate as to what could possibly count as a green job. Some argue that there are several different shades of green jobs.[2]

According to the US Department of Labor a "green" job is defined as a safe job, a secure job, and a job that pays a family-supporting wage.[3] Hmmm? Coal miners in Ohio make on average just over $64,000 per year, which is approximately $25,000 more than the state's average yearly income.[4] It is an above average family-supporting wage, secure and safe job that not only fuels our nation's energy supply but it also contributes greatly to the regional economy. Somehow I don't think the US department of labor considers a coal miner as a "green" job. But I digress.

The Obama administration, per its blog, declared that "green" jobs are skilled laborers who can install efficient heating and cooling systems and windows, who can retrofit homes to save electricity, who can build and install solar panels, wind turbines and other clean energy technologies.[5]

GreenJobs.com took an even narrower approach to the definition. According to their website a "green" job is a job or employment opportunity in the renewable energy sector worldwide.[6]

While the United States Conference of Mayors and the Mayors Climate Protection Center are for a wide construct for their definition:

*"Any activity that generates electricity using renewable or nuclear fuels, agriculture jobs supplying corn or soy for transportation fuels, manufacturing jobs producing goods used in renewable power generation, equipment dealers and wholesalers specializing in renewable energy or energy-efficiency products, construction and installation of energy and pollution management systems, government administration of environmental programs, and supporting jobs in the engineering, legal, research and consulting fields."[7] ~ **United States Conference of Mayors***

The United Nations Environment Programme (UNEP) defines "green" jobs as:

*"....work in agricultural, manufacturing, research and development (R&D), administrative, and service activities that contribute substantially to preserving or restoring environmental quality."~ **United Nations Environment Programme***

It's agonizingly clear that there is no consensus on what a green job actually is, because it appears the White House and the US Department of Labor can't even agree as to the definition. According to a Newsweek article entitled "What Green Jobs?" the working definition of "green" job is still open to interpretation and the very idea behind a green job ensures there will never be a full definition.[8] This does not sound very encouraging, given the major "green" job creation push the Obama administration, labor unions, GWAs and the UN has. Even the Bureau of Labor Statistics, which has been cogitating on the problem since last spring, hasn't made up its mind on how to count green jobs.[9]

Creating Millions of "Green" Jobs?

As I speak with friends both liberal and conservative alike about "green" jobs more often than not one question rises to the top. How can you create millions of something for which we have not yet defined? My basic response is of course, we can't, but that doesn't mean the government won't try. Furthermore, my publisher would have a stroke if I stopped this chapter for lack of clarity in this new jobs area. Therefore, I am forced to use the unclear and broad definition of "green" job used by the US Department of Labor (i.e. a green job is a safe job, a secure job, and a job that pays a family-supporting wage) for the purpose of the remaining text.[10]

Proponents maintain that millions of "green" jobs can be created with a simple government investment. Estimates range from anywhere from 1 million to as many as 40 million "green" jobs can be created by 2030.[11] I don't know about you but those numbers seemed farfetched to me, so I did a little digging to determine what those estimates were based on and are they reliable? My research yielded some interesting facts.

A study titled Green Jobs Myths published jointly by researchers at the University of Illinois and Case Western Reserve University found that most "green" jobs estimates include huge numbers of clerical, bureaucratic, and administrative positions which do not produce goods and services for consumption. In addition the report noted "green" job estimates use poor economic models based on dubious assumptions.[12]

Example: one estimate envisions a 4-fold increase in hydropower production jobs that can be created by 2018. The reality is that currently there are no shovel ready projects or even project blueprints that could if coupled with existing hydropower plants accommodate such an ambitious increase in employment opportunities or job growth of that magnitude in the arena of hydropower. An additional dilemma that must be factored into the equation is the open push for the elimination of existing hydropower sites due to environmental alarmist concerns.[13] This example gives standing to five major problems researchers of the study found with these overly optimistic forecasts:

"First, many of the sectors declared to be green are extremely small and even quite minor changes in capacity produce large percentage increases in growth.

Second, the growth rates forecast are huge by any standard, thus raising questions regarding their reliability.

Third, the green jobs literature exhibits a selective technological optimism, assuming away any problems that might slow adoption of favored technologies while ignoring the likelihood of technological improvements of disfavored ones.

Fourth, because many industries discussed as major drivers of green jobs are small and new, no official, vetted statistics are available.

*Finally, the reports often assert results that appear precise, giving the illusion of scientific certainty."~ **Green Jobs Myths**[14]*

Now with a clear definition lacking and obvious flaws in estimation models we see an observable pattern emerging, The Obama administration and the GWA's are no strangers to conflicting and exaggerated data which seems to be a recurring theme. Yet I digress. The next question would be has anyone tried this before?

President Obama and other politicians have held up Spain as a model for how the US government can create "green" jobs, yet, in March 2009 Universidad Rey Juan Carlos, one of Spain's leading universities, published a report on government aid to the renewable energy sector and its effects on employment. That report dealt a blow to the idea that government is the answer when it comes to expanding job growth as it relates to renewable energy. Tony Blankley in his Rasmussen Report "Economic Reality of 5 Million Green Jobs" noted that this study really marks the first time a critical analysis was done of the actual performance and impact government aid to the renewable energy sector has. He further noted it [Spanish Report] demonstrates that the Spanish "green jobs" agenda much like the agenda being pushed in the U.S. in fact destroys jobs.[15]

A core finding of the Spain report or the Spain experience was that for every "green" job created a loss of at least 2.2 regular jobs was felt on average, or about 9 jobs lost for every 4 "green" jobs created. Spain created 50,000 green jobs, and lost 110,000 regular jobs.[16] Moreover, the report exposed the average cost of one of those newly created "green" jobs was $800,000 US dollars. Wind industry jobs created during the same time period in Spain required subsidies of $1.4 million per job.[17] A recent study of wind energy in Denmark by a Danish think-tank CEPOS, found that each wind energy job created in Denmark costs the Denmark government $90,000 to $140,000 annually and was clearly unsustainable. The Danish research found once the government subsidies end the jobs end.[18]

Spain created an alarmingly low number of jobs given the expense. Of which only 10% percent of the "green" jobs were permanent.[19] It is painfully obvious that Green jobs and policies have been a disaster for Spain. Don't believe me? Unemployment in Spain currently stands at 19.3%[20] and reports estimate unemployment in Spain could reach as high as 25% within three years.[21]

Now the GWA and proponents of warming hysteria predicting the coming apocalypse will say, "That was Spain and we here in the good old US of A can do it better." Really? I thought I would look into that statement. Let's take a look at California. California has been the U.S. leader in pursuing a "green" jobs agenda and yet it has the highest unemployment and energy costs of any other state in the union. According to the US Bureau of Labor Statistic, since 2000 California's average unemployment rate has consistently topped the national average.[22] While California's average unemployment rate is presently 12.3% compared to Spain's 19.3%, I'm sure it doesn't feel any better.

"Green" Jobs Are Union Jobs?

The year 2009 provided a clear view into the link between Global Warming Alarmist (GWA), Unions and the real dogma behind "green" jobs. In February 2009 John Sweeney, President of the AFL-CIO announced a new Center for Green Jobs which was described as a "think-do tank" that will be a one-stop shop for information and technical assistance on public policy, consortium development, workforce and economic development programs, economic analysis and even curriculum development.[23] Why would that be significant given the center just wants to retrain unemployed workers for jobs? Let's look at the centers mission which is:

"The mission of the center is not only to engage public policy but to also move beyond that to help our labor unions implement real green jobs initiatives—initiatives that retain and create good union jobs, provide pathways to those jobs and assist with the design and implementation of training programs to prepare incumbent workers as well as job seekers for these family-sustaining careers."[24] ~ ***AFL-CIO***

Based on their mission statement they only want to retain and or create "green" union jobs, "…implement real green jobs initiatives—initiatives that retain and create good union jobs…" Hmmm?

A year earlier the United Steelworkers and green educators from the University of Cincinnati called a town meeting to announce a push for 20,000 new "green" jobs for union members that had been laid off or fired from manufacturing jobs.[25] The event sponsored by the Blue Green Alliance, a partnership between labor unions and environmental organizations, was billed as a way for laid-off workers from the Ford Plant in Batavia to get back on their feet.[26]

BlueGreen Alliance's focus according to their website is on turning blue collar jobs green. It has been their mission for several years.

"Launched in 2006 by the United Steelworkers and the Sierra Club, this unique labor-environmental collaboration has grown to include the Communications Workers of America (CWA), Natural Resources Defense Council (NRDC), Service Employees International Union (SEIU), Laborers' International Union of North America (LIUNA), Utility Workers Union of America (UWUA), American Federation of Teachers (AFT) and the Amalgamated Transit Union. The Blue Green Alliance unites more than eight million people in pursuit of good jobs, a clean environment and a green economy." ~ **BlueGreen Alliance**

It is quite obvious that unions see "green" jobs as a way to boost membership, which had been declining steadily since 1983, the first year comparable data was available for unions.[27] According to the US Bureau of Labor Statistic in 1983, union membership was 20.1% of the employed wage and salary workers. As of 2008 union membership is 12.4% of the employed wage and salary workers.[28] This is an increase from 12.1% in 2007 when the real push by the unions for "green" jobs became more active.

Of course we cannot forget the "green" money. In chapter 3 I explained that scientists have become dependent on a fear based support system with focus on perpetuating the problem to gather funding, rather than solving the problem. Well the allure of grant money for labor organization is no different. All promoted by the US Department of Labor.

In January 2010 Secretary of Labor Hilda L. Solis of the US Department of Labor announced the release of $100M in grants funded by the American Recovery and Reinvestment Act (stimulus bill) to support "green" job training programs.[29]

"Grant recipients are expected to work in conjunction with a diverse range of partners, including labor organizations, employers and workforce investment boards."[30] ~ **US Department of Labor**

The grants are given to help dislocated workers and others, including veterans, women, African Americans and Latinos, find jobs in expanding green industries and related occupations. Why not assist workers to just find any job, why must it be limited to green industries. With that said here is a list of some of the organizations that received funds from the US Department of Labor[31]:

* Utility Workers Union of America (UWUA), AFLCIO $4,993,922
* Blue Green Alliance (members largely unions) $5,000,000
* United Auto Workers (UAW) Labor Employment and Training Corporation $3,200,000
* SEIU Family of Funds (disguised as "HCAP, Inc.") $4,637,551
* International Transportation Learning Center (board consists almost exclusively of union leaders) $5,000,000
* International Brotherhood of Electrical Workers and the National Electrical Contractors Association $5,000,000
* Institute for Career Development (United Steelworkers) $4,658,983
* Communications Workers of America $3,969,056
* Thomas Shortman Training Scholarship and Safety Fund (SEIU) $2,802,269

It is no doubt that some jobs will be created, with these funds, Spain also created jobs. But why would unions want to promote the creation of jobs for only union members and not all Americans, while at the same time dismantling non-union jobs? Could it be to focus on perpetuating the problem to gather funding? Hmmm?

Kevin Jackson, a friend, popular pundit and blogger with his own radio show said to me in a phone conversation, "there are no green jobs, just jobs." He explained that in the past tube televisions were big bulky and took lots of energy, now we have ultra thin energy efficient televisions and those jobs were not green, they were just jobs.

By no stretch of the imagination am I against creating jobs; on the contrary as an elected official I have and will continue to support and vote for economic development projects that create jobs and I do believe workforce development centers greatly assist workers seeking employment. However I am firmly against limiting the scope of centers to focus on what I believe to be a limited and flawed ideology.

Re-training and re-education is a basic practice for unemployed workers, and I say let's do it, as long as it is being done in the name of creating productivity in the economy and not for express purpose of pursuing an ideology, or as a way to boost membership or for the sake of just saying we are creating jobs.

The reality is that in a future envisioned by the GWA's and the unions in order to get that good paying job, in order to live on a planet that you helped to save rather than one you are hell bent on destroying you better be prepared to swear an oath to the mighty unions and the Global Warming Alarmists, at least that is what they believe.

***

5

Chapter Five:
Fire and Ice, Really!

*Journalists have warned of climate change for 100 years,
but can't decide whether we face an ice age or warming.*

By
R. Warren Anderson, Research Analyst
Dan Gainor, Boone Pickens Free Market Fellow

I t was five years before the turn of the century and major media were warning of disastrous climate change. Page six of The New York Times was headlined with the serious concerns of "geologists." Only the president at the time wasn't Bill Clinton; it was Grover Cleveland. And the Times wasn't warning about global warming – it was telling readers the looming dangers of a new ice age.

The year was 1895, and it was just one of four different time periods in the last 100 years when major print media predicted an impending climate crisis. Each prediction carried its own elements of doom, saying Canada could be "wiped out" or lower crop yields would mean "billions will die."

Just as the weather has changed over time, so has the reporting – blowing hot or cold with short-term changes in temperature.

Following the ice age threats from the late 1800s, fears of an imminent and icy catastrophe were compounded in the 1920s by Arctic explorer Donald MacMillan and an obsession with the news of his polar expedition. As the Times put it on Feb. 24, 1895, "Geologists Think the World May Be Frozen Up Again."

Those concerns lasted well into the late 1920s. But when the earth's surface warmed less than half a degree, newspapers and magazines responded with stories about the new threat. Once again the Times was out in front, cautioning "the earth is steadily growing warmer."

After a while, that second phase of climate cautions began to fade. By 1954, Fortune magazine was warming to another cooling trend and ran an article titled "Climate – the Heat May Be Off." As the United States and the old Soviet Union faced off, the media joined them with reports of a more dangerous Cold War of Man vs. Nature.

The New York Times ran warming stories into the late 1950s, but it too came around to the new fears. Just three decades ago, in 1975, the paper reported: "A Major Cooling Widely Considered to Be Inevitable."

That trend, too, cooled off and was replaced by the current era of reporting on the dangers of global warming. Just six years later, on Aug. 22, 1981, the Times quoted seven government atmospheric scientists who predicted global warming of an "almost unprecedented magnitude."

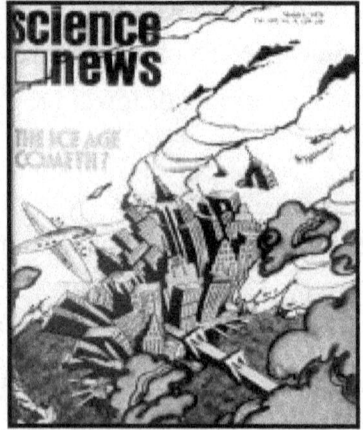

The future looked cold and ominous in this Science News depiction from March 1, 1975.

In all, the print news media have warned of four separate climate changes in slightly more than 100 years – global cooling, warming, cooling again, and, perhaps not so finally, warming. Some current warming stories combine the concepts and claim the next ice age will be triggered by rising temperatures – the theme of the 2004 movie "The Day After Tomorrow."

Recent global warming reports have continued that trend, morphing into a hybrid of both theories. News media that once touted the threat of "global warming" have moved on to the more flexible term "climate change." As the Times described it, climate change can mean any major shift, making the earth cooler or warmer. In a March 30, 2006, piece on ExxonMobil's approach to the environment, a reporter argued the firm's chairman "has gone out of his way to soften Exxon's public stance on climate change." The effect of the idea of "climate change" means that any major climate event can be blamed on global warming, supposedly driven by mankind.

Spring 2006 has been swamped with climate change hype in every type of media – books, newspapers, magazines, online, TV and even movies.

One-time presidential candidate Al Gore, a patron saint of the environmental movement, is releasing "An Inconvenient Truth" in book and movie form, warning, "Our ability to live is what is at stake."

Despite all the historical shifting from one position to another, many in the media no longer welcome opposing views on the climate. CBS reporter Scott Pelley went so far as to compare climate change skeptics with Holocaust deniers.

"If I do an interview with [Holocaust survivor] Elie Wiesel," Pelley asked, "am I required as a journalist to find a Holocaust denier?" he said in an interview on March 23 with CBS News's PublicEye blog.

He added that the whole idea of impartial journalism just didn't work for climate stories. "There

Time magazine's June 24, 1974, story showed how Arctic snow and ice had grown from 1968 to 1974.

becomes a point in journalism where striving for balance

becomes irresponsible," he said.

Pelley's comments ignored an essential point: that 30 years ago, the media were certain about the prospect of a new ice age. And that is only the most recent example of how much journalists have changed their minds on this essential debate.

Some in the media would probably argue that they merely report what scientists tell them, but that would be only half true.

Journalists decide not only what they cover; they also decide whether to include opposing viewpoints. That's a balance lacking in the current "debate."

This isn't a question of science. It's a question of whether Americans can trust what the media tell them about science.

Global Cooling: 1954-1976

The ice age is coming, the sun's zooming in Engines stop running, the wheat is growing thin A nuclear era, but I have no fear 'Cause London is drowning, and I live by the river **-- The Clash "London Calling," released in 1979**

The first Earth Day was celebrated on April 22, 1970, amidst hysteria about the dangers of a new ice age. The media had been spreading warnings of a cooling period since the 1950s, but those alarms grew louder in the 1970s.

A New York Times-line

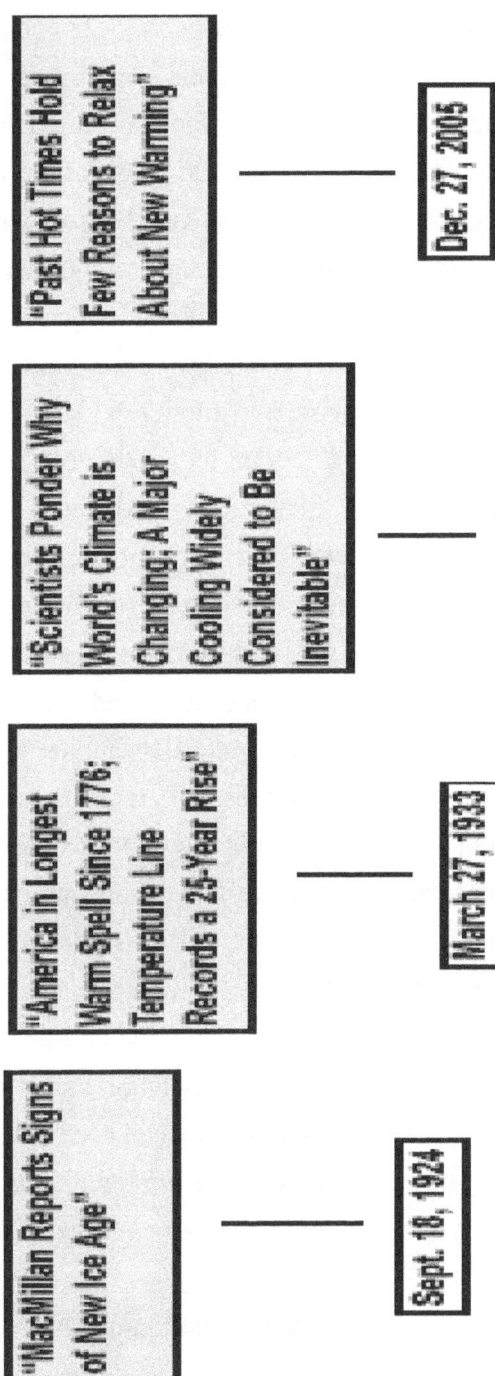

"MacMillan Reports Signs of New Ice Age"

Sept. 18, 1924

"America in Longest Warm Spell Since 1776; Temperature Line Records a 25-Year Rise"

March 27, 1933

"Scientists Ponder Why World's Climate is Changing; A Major Cooling Widely Considered to Be Inevitable"

May 21, 1975

"Past Hot Times Hold Few Reasons to Relax About New Warming"

Dec. 27, 2005

FIRE AND ICE, REALLY!   57

Three months before, on January 11, The Washington Post told readers to "get a good grip on your long johns, cold weather haters – the worst may be yet to come," in an article titled "Colder Winters Held Dawn of New Ice Age." The article quoted climatologist Reid Bryson, who said "there's no relief in sight" about the cooling trend. Journalists took the threat of another ice age seriously.

Fortune magazine actually won a "Science Writing Award" from the American Institute of Physics for its own analysis of the danger. "As for the present cooling trend a number of leading climatologists have concluded that it is very bad news indeed," Fortune announced in February 1974. "It is the root cause of a lot of that unpleasant weather around the world and they warn that it carries the potential for human disasters of unprecedented magnitude," the article continued. That article also emphasized Bryson's extreme doomsday predictions. "There is very important climatic change going on right now, and it's not merely something of academic interest." Bryson warned, "It is something that, if it continues, will affect the whole human occupation of the earth – like a billion people starving.

The effects are already showing up in a rather drastic way." However, the world population increased by 2.5 billion since that warning. Fortune had been emphasizing the cooling trend for 20 years. In 1954, it picked up on the idea of a frozen earth and ran an article titled "Climate – the Heat May Be Off."

The story debunked the notion that "despite all

you may have read, heard, or imagined, it's been growing cooler – not warmer – since the Thirties." The claims of global catastrophe were remarkably similar to what the media deliver now about global warming. "The cooling has already killed hundreds of thousands of people in poor nations," wrote Lowell Ponte in his 1976 book "The Cooling." If the proper measures weren't taken, he cautioned, then the cooling would lead to "world famine, world chaos, and probably world war, and this could all come by the year 2000."

There were more warnings. The Nov. 15, 1969, "Science News" quoted meteorologist Dr. J. Murray Mitchell Jr. about global cooling worries. "How long the current cooling trend continues is one of the most important problems of our civilization," he said. If the cooling continued for 200 to 300 years, the earth could be plunged into an ice age, Mitchell continued.

Six years later, the periodical reported "the cooling since 1940 has been large enough and consistent enough that it will not soon be reversed." A city in a snow globe illustrated that March 1, 1975, article, while the cover showed an ice age obliterating an unfortunate city.

In 1975, cooling went from "one of the most important problems" to a first-place tie for "death and misery." "The threat of a new ice age must now stand alongside nuclear war as a likely source of wholesale death and misery for mankind," said Nigel Calder, a former editor of "New Scientist."

He claimed it was not his disposition to be a "doomsday man." His analysis came from "the facts [that] have emerged" about past ice ages, according to the July/ August International Wildlife Magazine. The idea of a worldwide deep freeze snowballed.

Naturally, science fiction authors embraced the topic. Writer John Christopher delivered a book on the coming ice age in 1962 called "The World in Winter." In Christopher's novel, England and other "rich countries of the north" broke down under the icy onslaught. "The machines stopped, the land was dead and the people went south," he explained.

James Follett took a slightly different tack. His book "Ice" was about "a rogue Antarctic iceberg" that "becomes a major world menace." Follett in his book conceived "the teeth chattering possibility of how Nature can punish those who foolishly believe they have mastered her."

Global Warming: 1929-1969

Today's global warming advocates probably don't even realize their claims aren't original. Before the cooling worries of the '70s, America went through global warming fever for several decades around World War II.

The nation entered the "longest warm spell since 1776," according to a March 27, 1933, New York Times headline. Shifting climate gears from ice to heat, the Associated Press article began "That next ice age, if one is

A Time Magazine Time-line

Sept. 10, 1923

"The discoveries of changes in the sun's heat and the southward advance of glaciers in recent years have given rise to conjectures of the possible advent of a new ice age."

Jan. 2, 1939

"Gaffers who claim that winters were harder when they were boys are quite right... weather men have no doubt that the world at least for the time being is growing warmer."

June 24, 1974

"Climatological Cassandras are becoming increasingly apprehensive, for the weather aberrations they are studying may be the harbinger of another ice age."

April 9, 2001

"[S]cientists no longer doubt that global warming is happening, and almost nobody questions the fact that humans are at least partly responsible."

FIRE AND ICE, REALLY!   61

coming … is still a long way off."

One year earlier, the paper reported that "the earth is steadily growing warmer" in its May 15 edition. The Washington Post felt the heat as well and titled an article simply "Hot weather" on August 2, 1930. That article, reminiscent of a stand-up comedy routine, told readers that the heat was so bad, people were going to be saying, "Ah, do you remember that torrid summer of 1930. It was so hot that * * *."

The Los Angeles Times beat both papers to the heat with the headline: "Is another ice age coming?" on March 11, 1929. Its answer to that question: "Most geologists think the world is growing warmer, and that it will continue to get warmer." Meteorologist J. B. Kincer of the federal weather bureau published a scholarly article on the warming world in the September 1933 "Monthly Weather Review." The article began discussing the "wide-spread and persistent tendency toward warmer weather" and asked "Is our climate changing?" Kincer proceeded to document the warming trend. Out of 21 winters examined from 1912-33 in Washington, D.C., 18 were warmer than normal and all of the past 13 were mild.

New Haven, Conn., experienced warmer temperatures, with evidence from records that went "back to near the close of the Revolutionary War," claimed the analysis. Using records from various other cities, Kincer showed that the world was warming.

British amateur meteorologist G. S. Callendar made

a bold claim five years later that many would recognize now. He argued that man was responsible for heating up the planet with carbon dioxide emissions – in 1938.

It wasn't a common notion at the time, but he published an article in the Quarterly Journal of the Royal Meteorological Society on the subject. "In the following paper I hope to show that such influence is not only possible, but is actually occurring at the present time," Callendar wrote. He went on the lecture circuit describing carbon-dioxide-induced global warming.

But Callendar didn't conclude his article with an apocalyptic forecast, as happens in today's global warming stories. Instead he said the change "is likely to prove beneficial to mankind in several ways, besides the provision of heat and power." Furthermore, it would allow for greater agriculture production and hold off the return of glaciers "indefinitely."

On November 6 the following year, The Chicago Daily Tribune ran an article titled "Experts puzzle over 20 year mercury rise." It began, "Chicago is in the front rank of thousands of cities thuout [sic] the world which have been affected by a mysterious trend toward warmer climate in the last two decades."

The rising mercury trend continued into the '50s. The New York Times reported that "we have learned that the world has been getting warmer in the last half century" on Aug. 10, 1952. According to the Times, the evidence was the introduction of cod in the Eskimo's diet – a fish they had not encountered before 1920 or so. The following year, the paper reported that studies confirmed summers and winters were getting warmer.

This warming gave the Eskimos more to handle than cod. "Arctic Findings in Particular Support Theory of Rising Global Temperatures," announced the Times during the middle of winter, on Feb. 15, 1959. Glaciers were melting in Alaska and the "ice in the Arctic ocean is about half as thick as it was in the late nineteenth century."

A decade later, the Times reaffirmed its position that "the Arctic pack ice is thinning and that the ocean at the North Pole may become an open sea within a decade or two," according to polar explorer Col. Bernt Bachen in the Feb. 20, 1969, piece.

One of the most surprising aspects of the global warming claims of the 20th Century is that they followed close behind similar theories of another major climate change – that one an ice age.

Global Cooling: 1895-1932

The world knew all about cold weather in the 1800s. America and Europe had escaped a 500-year period of cooling, called the Little Ice Age, around 1850. So when the Times warned of new cooling in 1895, it was a serious prediction.

On Feb. 24, 1895, the Times announced "Geologists Think the World May Be Frozen Up Again." The article debated "whether recent and long-continued observations do not point to the advent of a second glacial period." Those concerns were brought on by increases in northern glaciers and in the severity of Scandinavia's climate.

Fear spread through the print media over the next three decades. A few months after the sinking of the Titanic, on Oct. 7, 1912, page one of the Times reported, "Prof. Schmidt Warns Us of an Encroaching Ice Age." Scientists knew of four ice ages in the past, leading Professor Nathaniel Schmidt of Cornell University to conclude that one day we will need scientific knowledge "to combat the perils" of the next one. The same day the Los Angeles Times ran an article about Schmidt as well, entitled "Fifth ice age is on the way." It was subtitled "Human race will have to fight for its existence against cold."

That end-of-the-world tone wasn't unusual. "Scientist says Arctic ice will wipe out Canada," declared a front-page Chicago Tribune headline on Aug. 9, 1923. "Professor Gregory" of Yale University stated that "another world ice-epoch is due." He was the American representative to the Pan-Pacific Science Congress and warned that North America would disappear as far south as the Great Lakes, and huge parts of Asia and Europe would be "wiped out." Gregory's predictions went on and on. Switzerland would be "entirely obliterated," and parts of South America would be "overrun." The good news – "Australia has nothing to fear." The Washington Post picked up on the story the following day, announcing "Ice Age Coming Here."

Talk of the ice age threat even reached France. In a New York Times article from Sept. 20, 1922, a penguin found in France was viewed as an "ice-age harbinger." Even though the penguin probably escaped from the Antarctic explorer Sir Ernest Shackleton's ship, it "caused considerable consternation in the country."

Some of the sound of the Roaring '20s was the noise of a coming ice age – prominently covered by The New York Times. Capt. Donald MacMillan began his Arctic expeditions in 1908 with Robert Peary. He was going to Greenland to test the "Menace of a new ice age," as the Times reported on June 10, 1923.

The menace was coming from "indications in Arctic that have caused some apprehension." Two weeks later the Times reported that MacMillan would get data to help determine "whether there is any foundation for the theory which has been advanced in some quarters that another ice age is impending."

On July 4, 1923, the paper announced that the "Explorer Hopes to Determine Whether new 'Ice Age' is Coming." The Atlanta Constitution also had commented on the impending ice age on July 21, 1923. MacMillan found the "biggest glacier" and reported on the great increase of glaciers in the Arctic as compared to earlier measures. Even allowing for "the provisional nature of the earlier surveys," glacial activity had greatly augmented, "according to the men of science." Not only was "the world of science" following MacMillan, so too were the "radio fans."

The Christian Science Monitor reported on the potential ice age as well, on July 3, 1923. "Captain Mac-Millan left Wicasset, Me., two weeks ago for Sydney, the jumping-off point for the north seas, announcing that one of the purposes of his cruise was to determine whether there is beginning another 'ice age,' as the advance of glaciers in the last 70 years would seem to indicate."

Then on Sept. 18, 1924, The New York Times declared the threat was real, saying "MacMillan Reports Signs of New Ice Age."

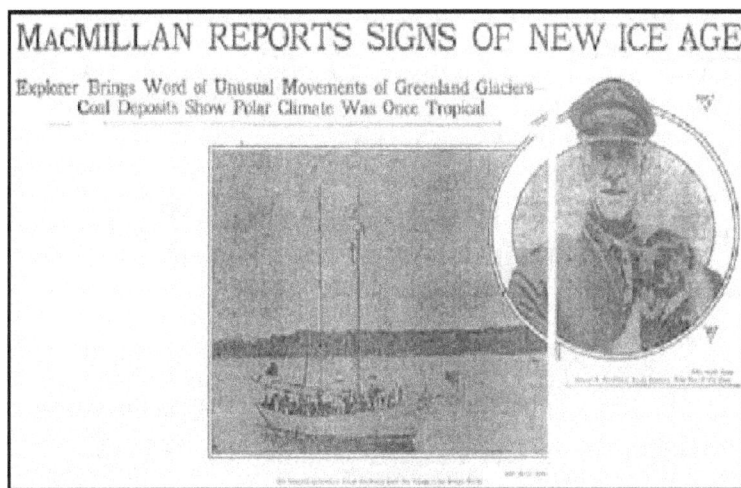

MacMILLAN REPORTS SIGNS OF NEW ICE AGE

Explorer Brings Word of Unusual Movements of Greenland Glaciers
Coal Deposits Show Polar Climate Was Once Tropical

Concerns about global cooling continued. Swedish scientist Rutger Sernander also forecasted a new ice age. He headed a Swedish committee of scientists studying "climatic development" in the Scandinavian country.

According to the LA Times on April 6, 1924, he claimed there was "scientific ground for believing" that the conditions "when all winds will bring snow, the sun cannot prevail against the clouds, and three winters will come in one, with no summer between," had already begun.

That ice age talk cooled in the early 1930s. But The Atlantic in 1932 puffed the last blast of Arctic air in the article "This Cold, Cold World." Author W. J. Humphries compared the state of the earth to the state of the world before other ice ages. He wrote "If these things be true, it is evident, therefore that we must be just teetering on an ice age." Concluding the article he noted the uncertainty of such things, but closed with "we do know that the climatic gait of this our world is insecure and unsteady, teetering, indeed, on an ice age, however near or distant the inevitable fall."

Cooling and Warming
Both Threats to Food

Just like today, the news media were certain about the threat that an ice age posed. In the 1970s, as the world cooled down, the fear was that mankind couldn't grow enough food with a longer winter. "Climate Changes Endanger World's Food Output," declared a New York Times headline on Aug. 8, 1974, right in the heat of summer. "Bad weather this summer and the threat of more of it to come hang ominously over every estimate of the world food situation," the article began. It continued saying the dire consequences of the cooling climate created a deadly risk of suffering and mass starvation.

Various climatologists issued a statement that "the facts of the present climate change are such that the most optimistic experts would assign near certainty to major crop failure in a decade," reported the Dec. 29, 1974, New York Times. If policy makers did not account for this oncoming doom, "mass deaths by starvation and probably in anarchy and violence" would result.

Time magazine delivered its own gloomy outlook on the "World Food Crisis" on June 24 of that same year and followed with the article "Weather Change: Poorer Harvests" on November 11. According to the November story, the mean global surface temperature had fallen just 1 degree Fahrenheit since the 1940s. Yet this small drop "trimmed a week to ten days from the growing season" in the earth's breadbasket regions.

The prior advances of the Green Revolution that bolstered world agriculture would be vulnerable to the lower temperatures and lead to "agricultural disasters." Newsweek was equally downbeat in its article "The Cooling World." "There are ominous signs that the earth's weather

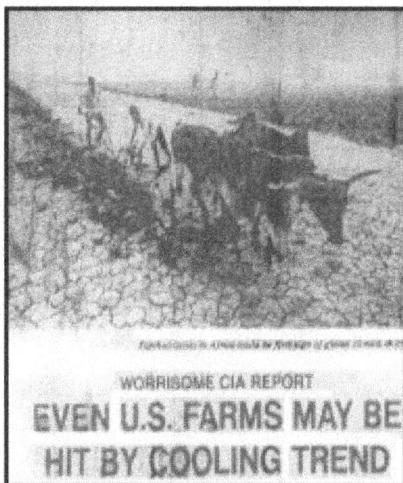

WORRISOME CIA REPORT

EVEN U.S. FARMS MAY BE HIT BY COOLING TREND

This headline from the May 31, 1976, U.S. News & World Report is a reminder that it hasn't been very long since global warming wasn't a concern.

patterns have begun to change dramatically," which would lead to drastically decreased food production, it said. "The drop in food output could begin quite soon, perhaps only ten years from now," the magazine told readers on April 28 the following year.

This, Newsweek said, was based on the "central fact" that "the earth's climate seems to be cooling down." Despite some disagreement on the cause and extent of cooling, meteorologists were "almost unanimous in the view that the trend will reduce agricultural productivity for the rest of the century."

Despite Newsweek's claim, agricultural productivity didn't drop for the rest of the century. It actually increased at an "annual rate of 1.76% over the period 1948 to 2002," according to the Department of Agriculture.

That didn't deter the magazine from warning about declining agriculture once again 30 years later – this time because the earth was getting warmer. "Livestock are dying. Crops are withering," it said in the Aug. 8, 2005, edition. It added that "extremely dry weather of recent months has spawned swarms of locusts" and they were destroying crops in France. Was global warming to blame? "Evidence is mounting to support just such fears," determined the piece.

U.S. News & World Report was agriculturally pessimistic as well. "Global climate change may alter temperature and rainfall patterns, many scientists fear, with uncertain consequences for agriculture." That was just 13 years ago, in 1993.

That wasn't the first time warming was blamed for influencing agriculture. In 1953 William J. Baxter wrote the book "Today's Revolution in Weather!" on the warming climate. His studies showed "that the heat zone is moving northward and the winters are getting milder with less snowfall."

Baxter titled a chapter in his book "Make Room For Trees, Grains, Vegetables and Bugs on the North Express!" The warming world led him to estimate that within 10 years Canada would produce more wheat than the United States, though he said America's corn dominance would remain. It was more than just crops that were in trouble. Baxter also noted that fishermen in Maine could catch tropical and semi-tropical fish, which were just beginning to appear. The green crab, which also migrated north, was "slowly killing" the profitable industry of steamer clams.

Ice, Ice Baby

Another subject was prominent whether journalists were warning about global warming or an ice age: glaciers. For 110 years, scientists eyed the mammoth mountains of ice to determine the nature of the temperature shift. Reporters treated the glaciers like they were the ultimate predictors of climate.

In 1895, geologists thought the world was freezing up again due to the "great masses of ice" that were frequently seen farther south than before. The New York Times reported that icebergs were so bad, and they decreased the temperature of Iceland so much, that inhabitants fearing a famine were "emigrating to North America."

In 1902, when Teddy Roosevelt became the first president to ride in a car, the Los Angeles Times delivered a story that should be familiar to modern readers. The paper's story on "Disappearing Glaciers" in the Alps said the glaciers were not "running away," but rather "deteriorating slowly, with a persistency that means their final annihilation."

The melting led to alpine hotel owners having trouble keeping patrons. It was established that it was a "scientific fact" that the glaciers were "surely disappearing." That didn't happen. Instead they grew once more.

More than 100 years after their "final annihilation" was declared, the LA Times was once again writing the same story. An Associated Press story in the Aug. 21, 2005, paper showed how glacier stories never really change. According to the article: "A sign on a sheer cliff wall nearby points to a mountain hut. It should have been at eye level but is more than 60 feet above visitors' heads. That's how much the glacier has shrunk since the sign went up 35 years ago."

But glacier stories didn't always show them melting away like ice cubes in a warm drink. The Boston Daily Globe in 1923 reported one purpose of MacMillan's Arctic expedition was to determine the beginning of the next ice age, "as the advance of glaciers in the last 70 years would indicate."

When that era of ice-age reports melted away, retreating glaciers were again highlighted. In 1953's "Today's Revolution in Weather!" William Baxter wrote that "the recession of glaciers over the whole earth affords the best proof that climate is warming," despite the fact that the world had been in its cooling phase for more than a decade when he wrote it. He gave examples of glaciers melting in Lapland, the Alps, Mr. Rainer and Antarctica.

Time magazine in 1951 noted permafrost in Russia was receding northward up to 100 yards per year. In 1952, The New York Times kept with the warming trend. It reported the global warming studies of climatologist Dr. Hans W. Ahlmann, whose "trump card" "has been the melting glaciers." The next year the Times said "nearly all the great ice sheets are in retreat."

U.S. News and World Report agreed, noted that "winters are getting milder, summers drier. Glaciers are receding, deserts growing" on Jan. 8, 1954. In the '70s, glaciers did an about face. Ponte in "The Cooling" warned that "The rapid advance of some glaciers has threatened human settlements in Alaska, Iceland, Canada, China, and the Soviet Union."

Time contradicted its 1951 report and stated that the cooling trend was here to stay. The June 24, 1974, article was based on those omnipresent "telltale signs" such as the "unexpected persistence and thickness of pack ice in the waters around Iceland."

Even The Christian Science Monitor in the same year noted "glaciers which had been retreating until 1940 have begun to advance." The article continued, "the North Atlantic is cooling down about as fast as an ocean can cool."

The New York Times noted that in 1972 the "mantle of polar ice increased by 12 percent" and had not returned to "normal" size. North Atlantic sea temperatures declined, and shipping routes were "cluttered with abnormal amounts of ice." Furthermore, the permafrost in Russia and Canada was advancing southward, according to the December 29 article that closed out 1974.

Decades later, the Times seemed confused by melting ice. On Dec. 8, 2002, the paper ran an article titled "Arctic Ice Is Melting at Record Level, Scientists Say." The first sentence read "The melting of Greenland glaciers and Arctic Ocean sea ice this past summer reached levels not seen in decades."

Was the ice melting at record levels, as the headline stated, or at a level seen decades ago, as the first line mentioned? On Sept. 14, 2005, the Times reported the recession of glaciers "seen from Peru to Tibet to Greenland" could accelerate and become abrupt.

This, in turn, could increase the rise of the sea level and block the Gulf Stream. Hence "a modern counterpart of the 18,000-year-old global-warming event could trigger a new ice age."

Government Comes to the Rescue

Mankind managed to survive three phases of fear about global warming and cooling without massive bureaucracy and government intervention, but aggressive lobbying by environmental groups finally changed that reality.

The Kyoto treaty, new emissions standards and foreign regulations are but a few examples. Getting the government involved to control the weather isn't a new concept. When the earth was cooling, The New York Times reported on a panel that recommended a multimillion-dollar research program to combat the threat.

That program was to start with $18 million a year in funding and increase to about $67 million by 1980, according to the Jan. 19, 1975, Times. That would be more than $200 million in today's dollars.

Weather warnings in the '70s from "reputable researchers" worried policy-makers so much that scientists at a National Academy of Sciences meeting "proposed the evacuation of some six million people" from parts of Africa, reported the Times on Dec. 29, 1974.

That article went on to tell of the costly and unnecessary plans of the old Soviet Union. It diverted time from Cold War activities to scheme about diverting the coming cold front. It had plans to reroute "large Siberian rivers, melting Arctic ice and damming the Bering Strait" to help warm the "frigid fringes of the Soviet Union."

Newsweek's 1975 article "The Cooling World" noted climatologists' admission that "solutions" to global cooling "such as melting the arctic ice cap by covering it with black soot or diverting arctic rivers," could result in more problems than they would solve.

More recently, 27 European climatologists have become worried that the warming trend "may be irreversible, at least over most of the coming century," according to Time magazine on Nov. 13, 2000. The obvious solution? Bigger government. They "should start planning immediately to adapt to the new extremes of weather that their citizens will face – with bans on building in potential flood plains in the north, for example, and water conservation measures in the south."

Almost 50 policy and research recommendations came with the report. The news media have given space to numerous alleged solutions to our climate problems. Stephen Salter of the University of Edinburgh had some unusual ideas to repel an effect of global warming. In 2002 he had the notion of creating a rainmaker, "which looks like a giant egg whisk," according to the Evening News of Edinburgh on Dec. 2, 2002.

The Atlantic edition of Newsweek on June 30, 2003, reported on the whisk. The British government gave him 105,000 pounds to research it. Besides promoting greater prosperity and peace, it could "lift enough seawater to lower sea levels by a meter, stemming the rise of the oceans – one of the most troublesome consequences of global warming." The rain created would be redirected toward land using the wind's direction.

Instead of just fixing a symptom of global warming, Salter now wants to head it off. He wants to spray water droplets into low altitude clouds to increase their whiteness and block out more sunlight. The National Academy of Sciences (NAS) has considered other ways to lower temperatures and the media were there to give them credence.

Newsweek on May 20, 1991, reported on five ways to fight warming from the National Research Council, the operating arm of the NAS. The first idea was to release "billions of aluminized, hydrogen-filled balloons" to reflect sunlight. To reflect more sunlight, "fire one-ton shells filled with dust into the upper atmosphere." Airplane engines could pollute more in order to release a "layer of soot" to block the sun. Should any sunlight remain, 50,000 orbiting mirrors, 39 square miles each, could block it out. With any heat left, "infrared lasers on mountains" could be used "to zap rising CFCs," rendering them harmless.

Global Warming: 1981-Present and Beyond

The media have bombarded Americans almost daily with the most recent version of the climate apocalypse. Global warming has replaced the media's ice age claims, but the results somehow have stayed the same – the deaths of millions or even billions of people, widespread devastation and starvation.

The recent slight increase in temperature could "quite literally, alter the fundamentals of life on the planet" argued the Jan. 18, 2006, Washington Post.
In the aftermath of Hurricane Katrina, Nicholas D. Kristof of The New York Times wrote a column that lamented the lack of federal spending on global warming. "We spend about $500 billion a year on a military budget, yet we don't want to spend peanuts to protect against climate change," he said in a Sept. 27, 2005, piece.

Kristof's words were noteworthy, not for his argument about spending, but for his obvious use of the term "climate change." While his column was filled with references to "global warming," it also reflected the latest trend as the coverage has morphed once again.

The two terms are often used interchangeably, but can mean something entirely different. The latest threat has little to do with global warming and has everything to do with … everything. The latest predictions claim that warming might well trigger another ice age.

The warm currents of the Gulf Stream, according to a 2005 study by the National Oceanography Centre in Southampton, U.K., have decreased 30 percent. This has raised "fears that it might fail entirely and plunge the continent into a mini ice age," as the Gulf Stream regulates temperatures in Europe and the eastern United States. This has "long been predicted" as a potential ramification of global warming.

Hollywood picked up on this notion before the study and produced "The Day After Tomorrow." In the movie global warming triggered an immediate ice age. People had to dodge oncoming ice. Americans were fleeing to Mexico. Wolves were on the prowl. Meanwhile our hero, a government paleoclimatologist, had to go to New York

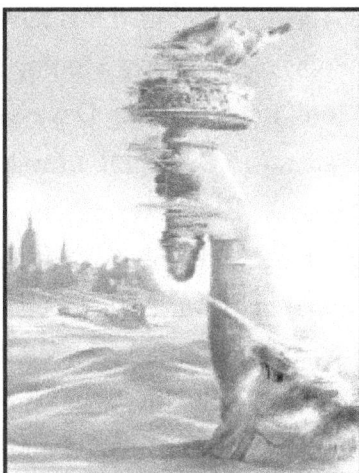

20th Century Fox's "The Day After Tomorrow" pushed the idea that global warming could lead to an ice age.

City to save his son from the catastrophe.

But it's not just a potential ice age. Every major weather event becomes somehow linked to "climate change." Numerous news reports connected Hurricane Katrina with changing global temperatures. Droughts, floods and more have received similar media treatment.

Even The New York Times doesn't go that far – yet. In an April 23, 2006, piece, reporter Andrew C. Revkin gave no credence to that coverage. "At the same time, few scientists agree with the idea that the recent spate of potent hurricanes, European heat waves, African drought and other weather extremes are, in essence, our fault. There is more than enough natural variability in nature to mask a direct connection, they say."

Unfortunately, that brief brush with caution hasn't touched the rest of the media. Time magazine's recent

cover story included this terrifying headline:
"Polar Ice Caps Are Melting Faster Than Ever... More And More; Land Is Being Devastated By Drought... Rising Waters Are Drowning Low-Lying Communities... By Any Measure, Earth Is At ... The Tipping Point The climate is crashing, and global warming is to blame. Why the crisis hit so soon —and what we can do about it"

That attitude reflects far more of the current media climate. As the magazine claimed, many of today's weather problems can be blamed on the changing climate. "Disasters have always been with us and surely always will be. But when they hit this hard and come this fast — when the emergency becomes commonplace —something has gone grievously wrong. That something is global warming," Time said.

Conclusion

What can one conclude from 110 years of conflicting climate coverage except that the weather changes and the media are just as capricious? Certainly, their record speaks for itself. Four separate and distinct climate theories targeted at a public taught to believe the news. Only all four versions of the truth can't possibly be accurate.

For ordinary Americans to judge the media's version of current events about global warming, it is necessary to admit that journalists have misrepresented the story three other times.

Yet no one in the media is owning up to that fact. Newspapers that pride themselves on correction policies for the smallest errors now find themselves facing a historical record that is enormous and unforgiving.

It is time for the news media to admit a consistent failure to report this issue fairly or accurately, with due skepticism of scientific claims.

***

This was reprinted with permission from the authors and the Business & Media Institute and division of the Media Research Center. More info can be found at http://www. mrc.org

6

Chapter Six:
Heretics, Really?

*"The dissenter is every human being at those moments of his life when he resigns momentarily from the herd and thinks for himself." ~ **Archibald Macleish***

T he greatest fear of the Global Warming Alarmists (GWA) is that people do in fact begin to separate from the herd and begin to think for themselves. After all, that is why I wrote this book and why you're almost certainly reading it. That is why the polish is slowly being dulled and why the GWA are scrambling to define those who have become skeptical about their prophecies of an impending doom. So, if you find yourself separated from the herd questioning the rhetoric filling our new digital world, Congratulation, you are a "dissenter" and you have joined the ranks of some of the world's greatest thinkers and scientific minds.

A dissenter is someone who rebels from established religious dogma; or one who disputes an accepted belief or doctrine, anyone who does not conform to an established attitude, doctrine, or principle.[1] After reading this definition my mind quickly turned to the parallels the GWA movement has with religious conviction. In recent years the GWA movement appears to have become more of a religion rather than a political issue. Example; GWA's have a god; mother earth, a bible the UN Intergovernmental Panel on Climate Change (IPCC) climate change report, evangelist Al Gore and others. It even has an apocalyptic end (the doomsday ending).

"The secular religion of global warming has all the elements of a religious faith: original sin (we are polluting the planet), ritual (separate your waste for recycling), redemption (renounce economic growth) and the sale of indulgences (carbon offsets). We are told that we must have faith (all argument must end, as Al Gore likes to say) and must persecute heretics (global warming skeptics are like Holocaust deniers, we are told)."[2]

"The belief of climate change, and that it is manmade, has become a pseudo-religion..."[3]

Don't believe me? Guy Dauncey, author and green activist proclaimed in his book *The Climate Challenge* that "climate change is Gaia's [goddess of the earth] message, saying time's up."[4] Hmmm?

Of course as with every religion there is dissent and stopping such dissent has been around for hundreds of years. History is riddled with dictators, kings and religious leaders who vowed to crush dissent. These leaders used claims of divine right to defeat dissent. That divine right they maintained was their right to lead and it came from God therefore, everyone must obey the same way they would obey God. Making dissent in any form viewed by theses leaders as heresy. This would leave dissenters de-monized and labelled as heretics subjecting them to lash-ings, banishment and even death. All these punitive meas-ures carried out for questioning the leaders will.

Today dictators don't claim divine right, they just "claim" and cling on to power by using intimidation and controlling the media. Example: In the country of Ertrea, all media is controlled by the Isayas Afewerki government and at least 10 journalists remain in prison after their arrests in 2001.[5] To quiet his critics President Hugo Chavez closed 32 radio stations, two television broadcasters and supported legislation to create prison sentences for people who com-mit "media crimes" in Venezuela.[6] In the country of Turk-menistan, political prisoners remain behind bars, all media is controlled by the government and the practice of religion is restricted.[7]

Granted, in third world countries we still see the days of lashing and even death have not been purged from the lexicon of punishment for dissenting, but it appears that in the US "Banishment" is holding strong as a useful tool in the arsenal against the global warming heretic.

According to Richard Lindzen, a Professor of Atmospheric Science at MIT, scientists who dissented from the GWA movement have seen their grant funds disappear and themselves labeled as industry stooges and scientific hacks.[8] Henk Tennekes was dismissed as research director of the Royal Dutch Meteorological Society after questioning the scientific underpinnings of global warming.[9] Aren't scientist suppose to question?

Aksel Winn-Nielsen, who is the former director of the U.N.'s World Meteorological Organization, was demonized as a tool of the coal industry for questioning the GWA movement. Two Italian professors Alfonso Sutera and Antonio Speranza after losing climate-research funding all but disappeared from the climate debate after raising questions.[10] Hmmm, aren't scientist suppose to raise questions?

Along with banishing those who dissent, from the global warming agenda, another common way of discrediting them falls under the category of name-calling or demonizing. The head of the U.N.'s IPCC climate chief dismissed global warming skeptics by insinuating they are in the pockets of big business and suggested they should go rub their faces in cancer-causing asbestos.[11] Bill Nye "The Science Guy," appearing on MSNBC's Rachel Maddow Show in Feb of 2010 brazenly labeled global warming skeptics as "unpatriotic."[12] The Boston Globe in a February 2007 article proclaimed that "global warming deniers are now on a par with Holocaust deniers."[13] Wow!

Again, we see that literal death is still not a viable option in the US for silencing the dissenter but in a close second place is "straight up putting a cap in 'em" (metaphorically speaking of course) to simply kill their reputations and careers. The Weather Channel's Heidi Cullen advocated for the American Meteorological Society to revoke their "Seal of Approval" from any television weatherman who expresses skepticism that human activity is creating global warming.[14] If you listen carefully you can hear the repeat of the metaphorical gun as it kills the professional careers of those who dare to deny or call in to question the dictates of the GWA.

Really? *"If a meteorologist can't speak to the fundamental science of climate change, then maybe the AMS shouldn't give them a Seal of Approval. Clearly, the AMS doesn't agree that global warming can be blamed on cyclical weather patterns,"[15] ~ **Heidi Cullen***

Our media instead of investigating and protecting, those being wronged are all too eager to be complicit in the destruction of the global warming dissenter.

"MRC's Free Market Project found that between January 1993 and October 1997 — a period leading up to the Kyoto conference that December — just 5% of global warming stories on the ABC, CBS, CNN and NBC evening newscasts mentioned the arguments of skeptical scientists, and 85% of stories did not even acknowledge the existence of scientific skeptics."[16]

*"From January 20 through April 22, 2001, as liberals were condemning President George W. Bush for his failure to push ratification of the Kyoto treaty, the ABC, CBS and NBC evening news shows completely excluded the views of global warming skeptics from their coverage, while just one story on CNN included a dissenter — **a 97% skew in favor of the doomsayers.**"[17]*

*"In early 2007, as Al Gore's An Inconvenient Truth was handed an Academy Award, the broadcast network morning news shows ramped up their global warming coverage. But skeptics were once again frozen out: MRC analysts found **just 3% of stories contained any mention of dissent from Gore's approach to global warming** — and even those were heavily stacked in favor of his "climate crisis" position."[18]*

HERETICS, REALLY?   87

These excerpts from the Media Research Center article on global warming and the media show a clear bias to the issue. Yet, after all has been said and done we are now seeing that the dissenters are correct. That the heretics perpetuating man's greatest gift, that of asking questions, speaking truth to power, is still alive and well.

In the Fourth Assessment Report (AR4), issued in 2007 by the U.N.'s Intergovernmental Panel on Climate Change (IPCC), scientists wrote that 40 percent of the Amazon rainforest in South America was endangered by global warming.[19] But that assertion was discredited when it emerged that the findings were written by a freelance journalist and green activist and it was based on a study by the World Wildlife Federation that had nothing to do with the issue of global warming.[20]

Even as I write this book skepticism has arisen about much of the information gathered for the United Nations panel which has recently required retraction or correction as well. The UN's IPCC has admitted that a claim made in its 2007 report that Himalayan glaciers could melt away by 2035 was unfounded.[21] This followed a New Scientist article revealing the source of the claim was not peer-reviewed scientific literature.[22]

So the question remains, does dissent matter, does it have a place in the Global Warming debate? The answer is simple, yes it does have a place. Where would we be if those who founded this great nation didn't rise and dissent? Where would we be if Martin Luther King, the great civil rights leader of this nation didn't rise up with conviction and dissent from the status quo? Where would we be on so many of the great issues not only here and now but throughout history if there were not individuals who had the courage to stand in the face of would be kings, dictators, leaders and question the dogma that is peddled as absolute truth? Free thinking would be criminalized at worst, marginalized at best to the point that idiocracy would end up as our ruler.

Dissent is frequently romanticized if you're on the left, and demonized and condemned if you're on the right. Dissent has been hijacked, twisted to meet the objectives of people who believe that you are too stupid to get it. It is a tool that they can use but one that you are not allowed to use. Dissent against the wars in Afghanistan and Iraq and you are labeled a true American. Dissent against Global Warming and you are labeled a moron..... Really?

***

7 Chapter Seven:
It Helps Minorities, Really?

"With all of the hysteria, all of the fear, all of the phony science, could it be that man-made global warming is the greatest hoax ever perpetrated on the American people? It sure sounds like it." ~ ***James M. Inhofe***

Global warming is no longer just an environmental issue; it has unfortunately morphed into an issue of race and civil rights. How and why you ask?

Over time some causes change identity and become linked to race and civil rights in some way. This is how supporters try to gather minorities, Americans of color to their cause. Let me explain. The same-sex marriage issue started out identified as "gay-marriage" and only came to national attention in 1994 in a particular Hawaiian court case which found that state's constitution could not prevent gay's equal marriage rights. It was just an issue of people wanting to show their love for one another and get married.[1]

*"Everyone with a beef, advocacy issue or pet project, invokes the image of black oppression in order to legitimize their case." ~ **Margaret Kimberley***

Now with the designation of "same-sex marriage" or "same-sex rights" politically correct and less offensive of course, it is now an issue of rights for a minority group of gay persons. Its supporters now proclaim it as a civil rights movement much like Americans of color in the 1950's and 1960's. Most Americans of color, as am I, are very offended by the comparison, but I digress.

The Global Warming Alarmist (GWA) movement has also morphed in much the same fashion. Knowing that Americans of color are sensitive to race issues, what better way to pull in more support than to pronounce that global warming can and does disproportionately affect Americans of color and it is akin to civil rights movement of the 50's and 60's. Further the designation and identity of the issue has changed from global warming to climate change (See Chapter 5).

A 2008 poll by the Commission to Engage African Americans on Climate Change, a brainchild of The Joint Center for Political and Economic Studies, found 81% of persons of color believe the federal government should take strong action to deal with global warming. Yet those polled were unwilling to shoulder any increases in energy prices.[2]

Just one year later a survey by the National Center for Public Policy Research found that 76% of Americans of color want a delay on climate change legislation at least until the economy recovers. This is a full reversal from the previous year. Additionally, the survey found 73% were again unwilling to shoulder any increases in energy prices and 38% believed that unemployment created by climate change legislation would impact Americans of color most.[3]

Those are some of the facts and statistics surrounding Global Warming as it relates to Americans of color but there are other factors that come into play. Misinformation and propaganda are some of the favorite tools of those engaged in a war. Now this isn't a conventional war with guns and bombs but make no mistake this is a war. But the guns have been replaced with "Myths" and the bombs have been replaced with "rumors."

I have heard so many myths concerning global warming and its effects on Americans of color. I have, to my astonishment, heard that George W. Bush caused hurricanes Katrina and Rita. Hmmm? Former President Bush sat in the oval office with a weather machine under his desk franticly pushing the button to create a hurricane to wipe out an entire American city. This of course is absurd. Yet it persists and is clearly a MYTH!

Second, several reports from GWA's organizations

believe that the six states, with the largest populations of Americans of color, Mississippi, Louisiana, Georgia, Maryland, South Carolina and Alabama are in the Atlantic hurricane alley and are expected to be inundated with more intense hurricanes and natural disasters, due to global warming.[4] They point to the fact hurricane Katrina displaced more than 700,000 Americans, and poor Americans of color represented a disproportionate percentage of those displaced, as proof that global warming is bad for Americans of color.[5] As plausible as they may want this to seem it does not stand up under further scrutiny.

While hurricanes and other natural disasters are very tragic, there is no definitive link between global warming and increased natural disasters. In fact it is now clear that the United Nations Intergovernmental Panel on Climate Change (IPCC), has wrongly linked global warming to an increase in the number and or severity of natural disasters. The IPCC report and claims were based on an unpublished report by Robert Muir-Wood the head of research at Risk Management Solutions, who was looking for link between increases in global monetary losses (cost) caused by weather-related disasters and social changes like growth in population.[6] The study, which was not subject to any scientific scrutiny, even its own authors later, withdrew its claim citing the evidence supporting such a claim was weak.[7]

"There have been repeated claims that this past year's hurricane activity was another sign of human-induced climate change.

Everything from the heat wave in Paris to heavy snows in Buffalo has been blamed on people burning gasoline to fuel their cars, and coal and natural gas to heat, cool and electrify their homes. Yet how can a barely discernible, one-degree increase in the recorded global mean temperature since the late 19th century possibly gain public acceptance as the source of recent weather catastrophes? And how can it translate into unlikely claims about future catastrophes?" [8]

Robert Muir-Wood's study found from 1950 to 2005 no increase in the cost impact of disasters once growth was accounted for yet, from 1970-2005 there was a 2% annual cost increase corresponded with a period of rising global temperatures.[9] The IPCC ran with just that selected data from the report. Robert Muir-Wood stated that some caveats exist with his findings; 1) monetary exchange rates which meant that disasters hitting the US would appear to cost more in insurance payouts, and 2) all the increase was accounted for by the strong hurricane seasons 2004 and 2005.[10]

Furthermore, according to the National Oceanic and Atmospheric Administration, Atlantic hurricane activity appears to have phases and within these multidecadal phases certain years will be influenced by factors such as El Niño or La Niña. This typically translates to fewer hurricanes in El Niño years and more in La Niña years.[11]

"There is still uncertainty as to whether global warming has affected hurricane frequency or intensity for a variety of reasons." ~ **National Oceanic and Atmospheric Administration**

It is also a commonly reported myth when discussing global warming and its impact on Americans of color, to cite heat-related deaths. GWA claim that global warming is expected to increase the frequency and intensity of heat waves or extreme heat events and given Americans of color suffer heat related deaths at greater rates than that of others and have half the rate of air conditioning penetration, as proof of this.[12]

These statements by GWAs are again plausible but only half truths. As previously explained there is no definitive link between global warming and increased natural disasters up to and including heat waves. In fact it is now clear that the IPCC has wrongly linked global warming to an increase in the number and or severity of any natural disasters. This of course does not diminish the fact that heat related deaths and air conditioning penetration rates are issues of importance to Americans of color and should be addressed. The recognition that this is perhaps more about economics and the affordability of electricity and air conditioners rather than the Global Warming boogeyman would be a great and honest start.

Another commonly reported myth is that Americans of color are at greater risk from energy price shock and spend thirty percent more of their income on energy than others.[13] This actually is not a myth. The survey noted above by the National Center for Public Policy Research revealed that 73% were unwilling to shoulder any increases in energy prices. In my research I wanted to know why? Looking deeper into the survey it revealed that only 67% of those surveyed were employed, 50% of those surveyed made a household income of $40,000 dollars or less per year and most had little or no college education.[14] Given that, it is clear that Americans of color will be at greater risk from energy prices given the low household income and lack of education.

This is the bottom line for Americans of color, these "environmentalists" are peddling a dream and we have all been preached to about the power of "The Dream." Only their dream is nothing more than a pack of lies, a bill of goods being sold to you as some kind of planetary utopia. A close inspection of the track that they are laying exposes just how weak their claims are becoming and prove that they are headed off the rails. The mistruths of this utopia need to be brought down to reality. I am truly amazed by the fact that supporters believe an equality or utopia can be achieved, furthermore the fact that the very solutions that they claim will reach this racial equality and cure environmental injustice just further inflame the injustice they desire to cure.

The utopia solution touted by the GWAs is a cap-and-trade or carbon trading system as described in chapter 3 of this book. According to the Heritage Foundation, under such a system the annual family-of-four energy cost will rise by $1,000 dollars, and the gasoline price will rise by more than $1.20 per gallon.[15] Further the annual increase cost associated with goods and services is expected to rise by more than $3,000 dollars.[16] I don't know about you but no middle class American household can afford that, not to mention middle class households of color. Those GWAs will simply brush this aside and they will claim it to be just a small amount, just a modest cost increase.

Really? *"American households will be most affected by energy costs, but even here the increase would be modest..." ~ Environmental Defense Fund*

GWAs also fail to mention to Americans of color the job losses that will occur. They peddle the fact that this "green" utopia for Americans of color will be flush with lots of jobs, great paying jobs. Of course as I explained in chapter 4 that nothing could be further from the truth.

The Heritage Foundation estimates job losses from a GWA cap-and-trade carbon tax system could exceed 2.5 million for several years.[17] What is even more disheartening about this mistruth is that the GWA know jobs losses will occur, yet chose not to convey this to Americans of color.

> *"...Total jobs loss would be minimal. The* **Really?** *manufacturing sector is projected to see some job losses, but the models show that losses due to an emission cap would be minimal..."* ~ ***Environmental Defense Fund***

Additionally, levels of employment for Americans of color lag far behind others even when the economy is booming. It can then be surmised that the unemployment figures for Americans of color will far exceed that of others in a recession.[18] Example, according to the Department of Labor the average unemployment rate in December 2009 is 10% while for Americans of color it is 16.2%.[19] Therefore it is clearly logical to assume that any job losses will adversely impact Americans of color most, given these lags in employment.

Now I have to ask myself why GWAs would promote to Americans of color mistruths about a promise of a green jobs utopia while knowing all along it will not come to pass. The answer is simple, because they need the community organizing skills of our people. We have proven our ability to fight for an individual, to fight for an issue, seek justice where there was injustice and fight for equality in the face of inequality. That my friend is why they are even, as I write this book, attempting to enlist Americans of color into their fight and why we as a people must understand that this fight is unbalanced, unequal and its goals for a utopia are not possible. In the GWA rush to protect the planet and create equality they are subjugating the very people they proclaim as their allies. The reality is that there will always be inequality. Thomas Sowell said it best in his essay *Race, Culture, And Equality*, "real income consists of output and output depends on inputs. These inputs are almost never equal – or even close to being equal"[20]

Sowell is right, how hard we work and how much we add to the system will never be equal to what is returned to us but the lesson here is not to quit or complain or be duped but to be smart and effective about what and about how we decide to "input" versus realistically what we expect out. What I do know and what I believe is that if we input truth, justice will inevitably be rendered. As Americans of color we must work and push for those things that hold truth, not those things that are based on lies, rumors and myths. We can lead the way and dream of a day where we close the gap of inequality by demanding an open and honest level playing field.

***

8

Chapter Eight:
Solutions, Really?

*"There is a positive solution to everything. Find it and you will find less stress." ~ **Catherine Pulsifer***

I
n today's political environment it almost feels as though positive solutions on any issue are a thing of the past. Global Warming Alarmist (GWA) considers only renewable energy forgoing any positive changes taking place with other energy sectors. As you will see their proposed solutions seem to only prohibit and prevent Americans from technologically advancing and enjoying the comforts we have come to know.

With that said GWAs have identified seven solutions to fix the global warming problem; a problem that is based on a hoax at worst and at best inferior science. I have coined the GWA plan the "Stop Plan."

Stop Denying: As I explained in chapter 6, denial is a part of what makes us great. Yet to GWAs denial is heresy, subject to a wide range of punitive actions that range from name calling to banishment. Those punishments can be avoided if you understand what sin you've committed. They propose the first step in their solution is to stop denying and admit your individual sin by calculating the amount of sin, i.e. "calculate your carbon footprint." This seemingly harmless endeavor allows you to see just how much CO_2 you are producing while living your current lifestyle. The thought is once you see how much damage you're doing to the planet, you will then take corrective action. I believe the goal is to guilt you in to accepting the so called truth, the one you were forced to accept.

Stop Using Fossil Fuels: The GWA movement believes the first major challenge is eliminating the burning and use of fossil fuels; coal, oil and eventually even natural gas.[1] They claim that global warming is a catastrophe and to stop it we need to shut down all the coal plants, oil refineries and natural gas platforms by 2020. There is even an online petition calling for a stop to the burning of fossil fuels whose goal is to get one million signatures. So far 44 have signed up.[2] Never mind that currently 84% of the energy consumed in the United States comes from fossil fuels, petroleum, coal and natural gas.[3] Never mind countless products are made in some form or fashion from fossil fuels. Never mind there are now clean technologies and clean projects that can reduce CO_2 emissions from fossil fuels.

"With CCTI's technology, coal becomes a cost-effective, efficient and extremely clean-burning fuel that could potentially reduce our dependency upon oil. Over time, as utilities, power plants and manufacturers shift to our clean coal, we can achieve major advances in reducing pollution throughout the globe, and become the worldwide emission standard for future plants" ~ **Clean Coal Technologies, Inc.**

Stop Traveling and Driving: Here in America cars and planes are at the cornerstone of mobility in our society, yet they are the root of all that is unholy, according to the hyperbole of the GWA. They want you to move closer to work, use mass transit only. They would further prefer you switch to walking, cycling or anything that does not require anything other than human energy.[4] Really?

They also want to restrict flying to only critical, long-distance trips.[5] If traveling is required GWAs recommend using other means-especially for short trips.[6] Yet they themselves can jet set around the globe preaching flawed science and predicting catastrophes.

"We could close every factory, lock away every car and turn off every light in the country, but it won't halt global warming if we carry on taking planes as often as we do." ~ Mark Lynas

Stop Parking: If GWAs can't stop you from driving, then they want you to stop parking. Sounds stupid? California state senate voted to regulate free parking throughout the state so that there would be less parking.[7] Less parking? The state senate believes it will lead to less driving, thereby forcing you out of your car because you can't find a place to park.

"Free parking has significant social, economic and environmental costs, it increases congestion and greenhouse gas emissions." ~ California State Senator Alan Lowenthal

Stop Shopping. Now this one threw me for a loop, because my wife would not have a hard time with this. REALLY! We are a nation of consumers. Purchasing is what drives our economy. Yet, proponents of global warming believe that the easiest way to cut back on greenhouse gas emissions is simply to buy less. Given most products are made from fossil fuels being burned to produce and ship these products GWAs believe, cutting the demand is the best way to kill the supply.[8]

Stop Eating Meat. GWAs believe that livestock animals raised for meat and dairy are responsible for 14% of the global warming problem.[9] They see that meat, whether beef, chicken or pork, requires shipping sometimes halfway across the globe thereby contributing to global warming CO_2 levels.[10] Don't believe me?

Really? *"Producing the annual beef diet of the average American emits as much greenhouse gas as a car driven more than 1,800 miles." ~ **February 2009 Scientific American Magazine***

There is a lot more on this floating around the net and I would encourage all of you carnivores to quickly hit the keyboard and check out exactly why this should concern you and why if nothing else has motivated you this should be the topic.

Stop Having Children. I kid you not. This idea has been floated by the GWA movement for years. There are 6.6 billion people living today, a number that is predicted to increase exponentially by mid-century.[11] So it is believed by the GWA's that in order to save the planet we need the government to impose limits on the number of children.

*"Ultimately, a one child per couple rule is not sustainable either and there is no perfect number for human population. But it is clear that more humans mean more greenhouse gas emissions." ~ **David Biello***

Stop, stop, stop! Next the GWA movement will declare all CO_2 illegal and require us to STOP breathing. Wait? The Obama Administration's EPA administrator Lisa Jackson declared that CO_2 threatens public health and the environment and the science overwhelmingly shows unprecedented levels due to human activity.[12] Hmmm?

Now I realize that this is a lot to take in. I realize that I have thrown a lot of information out there and that my opinion on this matter is very clear. Global Warming as it is being peddled to us, forced down our throats is nothing more than a scam that amounts to nothing more than another way of stealing money from not just American taxpayers but from people around the world.

As I sat down to write this book the wheels started to come off the Global Warming Bandwagon, literally. Phil Jones, the preeminent chief global warming scientist was interviewed by the BBC. Caught with his hand in the cookie jar he has made some astonishing revelations, here are just a few of the questions asked by the BBC and the answers given by Phil Jones:[13]

- Do you agree that according to the global temperature record used by the IPCC, the rates of global warming from 1860-1880, 1910-1940 and 1975-1998 were identical?

"...Temperature data for the period 1860-1880 are more uncertain, because of sparser coverage, than for later periods in the 20th Century. The 1860-1880 period is also only 21 years in length. As for the two periods 1910-40 and 1975-1998 the warming rates are not statistically significantly different (see numbers below). I have also included the trend over the period 1975 to 2009, which has a very similar trend to the period 1975-1998. So, in answer to the question, the warming rates for all 4 periods are similar and not statistically significantly different from each other."

- Do you agree that from 1995 to the present there has been no statistically-significant global warming?

"Yes..."

- Do you agree that from January 2002 to the present there has been statistically significant global cooling?

"No..."

- When scientists say "the debate on climate change is over", what exactly do they mean - and what don't they mean?

"It would be supposition on my behalf to know whether all scientists who say the debate is over are saying that for the same reason. I don't believe the vast majority of climate scientists think this. This is not my view. There is still much that needs to be undertaken to reduce uncertainties..."

- Would it be reasonable looking at the same scientific evidence to take the view that recent warming is not pre-dominantly manmade?

"No..."

Let's face it my friends, when asked direct questions by the Mainstream Media (FINALLY) the answers were what I expected. Warming trends are cyclical, long before you loaded up your SUV for a quick trip to the coffee shop, before heading to the mall the earth had gone through periods of warming followed by periods of some cooling. There is no "Consensus" among all scientists as to the claim that global warming is the result of manmade activities and it appears that the debate is now on an open and honest playing field.

Arm yourself with the truth, stand in the face of those preaching false doctrine and stand your ground my friends because this isn't just a fight over a degree or two. This remains a fight for our very freedom. Just take a look at our government today and ask yourself this simple question, are they working for you? Really?

***

Notes

CHAPTER 1: GLOBAL WARMING...REALLY?

1. Vijay Modi, "Improving Electricity Services in Rural India," The Earth Institute at Columbia University, December 2005

2. Joe Brock, "IEA sees 1.3 billion people without power in 2030," Reuters, November 10, 2009, http://www.reuters.com/article/idUS-TRE5A932Z20091110

3. Public Citizen.Org, "Environmental Statement on Nuclear Energy and Global Warming," 2005, http://www.citizen.org/documents/groupnucle-arstmt.pdf

4. US Energy Information Administration, "Annual Energy Review Report 2008," June 2009, http://tonto.eia.doe.gov/energyexplained/index.cfm

5. Ibid

6. Staff, "U.S. Renewable Energy Exceeds Nuclear Power," Environmental Leader.Com, July 30, 2009

7. Jeffery M. Jones, "Savings Trumps Environment for Making Homes Greener," Gallup, December 8, 2009, http://www.gallup.com/poll/124619/Savings-Trumps-Environment-Making-Homes-Greener.aspx

8. Ibid

9. Ibid

10. Newt Gingrich, "We Can Have Green Conservatism -- And We Should," Human Events.Com, April 23, 2007

11. National Oceanic and Atmospheric Administration (NOAA) National Climatic Data Center, "What is Global Warming?"

12. Ibid

13. Newt Gingrich, "We Can Have Green Conservatism -- And We Should," Human Events.Com, April 23, 2007

14. Ibid

15. Joseph Bast, "Global Warming Madness and How to Stop It Heartlander," The Heartland Institute, 02/01/2007

16. Joseph D'Aleo, "12 Facts about Global Climate Change That You Won't Read in the Popular Press," The Heartland Institute, August. 18, 2008

17. Drew Thornley, "Computer Models Fail to Predict Climate," The Heartland Institute, Febuary 1, 2008

18. Guy Dauncey, "The Climate Challenge," New Society Publishers, 2009

19. Dr. Tim Ball, "Completely inadequate IPCC models produce the ultimate deception about man-made global warming," Canada Free Press, December 22, 2008

20. National Aeronautics and Space Administration, "NASA Oceanography," http://nasascience.nasa.gov/earth-science/oceanography, retrieved 12/18/2009

21. Wolfgang Knorr, "Is the airborne fraction of anthropogenic CO_2 emissions increasing?," University of Bristol, UK, November 7, 2009

22. Tim Ball, "Pre-industrial CO_2 levels were about the same as today. How and why we are told otherwise?," Canada Free Press, December 10, 2008

23. Tim Ball, "Pre-industrial CO_2 levels were about the same as today. How and why we are told otherwise?," Canada Free Press, December 10, 2008

24. Ernst-George Beck, "180 Years of Atmospheric CO_2 Gas Analysis By Chemical Methods," Energy & Environment, 2007

25. Ernst-George Beck, "180 Years of Atmospheric CO_2 Gas Analysis By Chemical Methods," Energy & Environment, 2007

26. US Energy Information Administration, "Emissions of Greenhouse Gases in the United States 2008," December 2009, ftp://ftp.eia.doe.gov/pub/oiaf/1605/cdrom/pdf/ggrpt/057308.pdf

27. Clayton Sandell, "Climate:2009 Caps Hottest Decade on Record," ABC News, December 8, 2009, http://abcnews.go.com/Technology/climate-2009-hottest-year-record/story?id=9283733

28. Kathleen Hartnett White, "Climate Change & Carbon Dioxide (CO2) Regulation," Texas Public Policy Foundation, January 2009

29. Bob Ellis, "Nasa Study Shows Sun Responsible for Planet Warming," Dakota Voice, June 5, 2009

30. Ibid

31. National Oceanic and Atmospheric Administration, "Use Gases and Aerosols," National Oceanic and Atmospheric Administration Research programs that study Greenhouse Gases and Aerosols, http://www.oar.noaa.gov/climate/t_greenhouse.html

32. Ibid

33. Ibid

34. Sue Ann Bowling, "How Do Greenhouses Work," Alaska Science Forum, April 20, 1987

35. Ibid

36. National Oceanic and Atmospheric Administration, "Greenhouse Gases Frequently Asked Questions," December 9, 2009, http://lwf.ncdc.noaa.gov/oa/climate/gases.html#INTRO

37. Ibid

38. Dr. Tim Ball, "Politics of climate science: selective research, ignored facts," Canada Fee Press, July 27, 2009,

39. Christopher Booker, "Polar bear expert barred by global warmest," Telegraph.co.uk, June 27, 2009, http://www.telegraph.co.uk/comment/columnists/christopherbooker/5664069/Polar-bear-expert-barred-by-global-warmists.html

40. Ibid

41. Ibid

42. James Delingpole, "Polar bears in danger? Is this some kind of joke," The Times of London, November 12, 2007, http://www.timesonline.co.uk/tol/comment/columnists/guest_contributors/article2852551.ece

43. Jon Birger, "What if global-warming fears are overblown?," Fortune Magazine, May 14, 2009

44. Russell Jenkins, "British geographers find uncharted glaciers in Albania," The Times Online, January 29, 2010

45. Rasmussen Reports, "Americans Skeptical of Science Behind Global Warming," December 03, 2009

46. Consensus. "Merriam-Webster Online Dictionary. 2009. Merriam-Webster Online," December 17, 2009 <http://www.merriam-webster.com/dictionary/Consensus>

47. Association of American Physicians and Surgeons, "32,000 scientists dissent from global-warming consensus," May 20, 2008, http://www.aapsonline.org/newsoftheday/0026

48. U.S. Senate Committee on Environment & Public Works, "U. S. Senate Minority Report: More Than 700 International Scientists Dissent Over Man-Made Global Warming Claims," March 16, 2009, http://epw.senate.gov/public/index.cfm?FuseAction=Minority.Blogs&ContentRecord_id=2674E64F-802A-23AD-490B-BD9FAF4DCDB7

49. Marc Morano , "Update: 'Consensus' Takes Another Hit! More than 60 German Scientists Dissent Over Global Warming Claims! Call Climate Fears 'Pseudo 'Religion'; Urge Chancellor to 'reconsider' views," Climate Depot, August 04, 2009

CHAPTER 2: LEADERS FOR THE CAUSE, REALLY?

1. Lawrence Meyers, "Global Warming: Hypocrisy of the Alarmists"

2. Full text of Prince Charles's speech to the Copenhagen climate conference,http://www.guardian.co.uk/environment/2009/dec/15/prince-charles-speech- copenhagen- climate

3. Leadership. (2009). "Merriam-Webster Online Dictionary," Retrieved December 29, 2009, from http://www.merriam-webster.com/dictionary/leadership

4. Credibility. (2009). "Merriam-Webster Online Dictionary," Retrieved December 29, 2009, from http://www.merriam-webster.com/dictionary/credibility

5. Peter Roff, "Obama's SUV-Laden Motorcade Demonstrates His Climate Change Hypocrisy," June 22, 2009, U.S. News & World Report.

6. TCPR Staff, "Al Gore's Personal Energy Use Is His Own Inconvenient Truth," Tennessee Center for Policy Research, February 25, 2007.

7. Drew Johnson, "Carbon Credits Not All They're Cracked Up to Be," Tennessee Center for Policy Research, September 1, 2007.
Peter Schweizer, "Gore isn't quite as green as he's led the world to believe," USA Today, December 7, 2006 , http://www.usatoday.com/news/opinion/editorials/2006-08-09-gore-green_x.htm

8. James Taylor, "Chicago Mayor is scolded for Global Warming hypocrisy," The Heartland Institute, September 1, 2007

9. Rome Neal, "Storm Over Mass. Windmill Plan," CBS News, http://www.cbsnews.com/stories/2003/06/26/sunday/main560595.shtml.

10. Ibid

11. Rick Klein, "Kennedy faces fight on Cape Wind," The Boston Globe, April 27, 2006

12. Intergovernmental Panel of Climate Change Organizational Change, http://www.ipcc.ch/organization/organization.htm

13. Intergovernmental Panel on Climate Change, "Details of Outreach Activities carried out by Chairman IPCC," August 31, 2008

14. Ibid

15. Christopher Booker, "The questions Dr Pachauri still has to answer," Telegraph UK, December 26, 2009, http://www.telegraph.co.uk/comment/columnists/christopherbooker/6890839/The-questions-Dr-Pachauri-still-has-to-answer.html
Ajmer Singh, "Pachauri in a spot as climategate hits TERI," India Today, January 10, 2010, http://indiatoday.intoday.in/site/Story/78466/Pachauri+in+a+spot+as+climategate+hits+TERI.html?page=0

16. Ibid

17. Gilligan Andrew, "Copenhagen climate summit: 1,200 limos, 140 private planes and caviar wedges," Telegraph UK, December 5, 2009, http://www.telegraph.co.uk/earth/copenhagen-climate-change-confe/6736517/Copenhagen-climate-summit-1200-limos-140-private-planes-and-caviar-wedges.html

18. Sharyl Attkisson, "Copenhagen Summit Turned Junket?," CBS News, January 11, 2010

19. Lawrence Solomon, "Lawrence Solomon: Wikipedia's climate doctor," National Post, December 19, 2009

20. Joshua Rhett Miller, "Fraud in Europe's Cap and Trade System a 'Red Flag,' Critics Say," FoxNews, December 19, 2009

21. David Asman, "On Global Warming: Follow the Money Indeed!," Fox News, February 12, 2007

22. Staff Writer, "With five private jets, Travolta still lectures on global warming," London Evening Standard, March 30, 2007

23. Bill Vallicella, "Gore a Hypocrite, So No Global Warming?," Maverick Philosopher Blog, March 18, 2009

CHAPTER 3: THERE'S MONEY IN IT, REALLY?

1. Bret Stephens, "Climategate: Follow the Money," Wall Street Journal, December 1, 2009

2. Lewis Page, "CRU cherrypicked Russian climate data," The Register UK, December 17, 2009, http://www.theregister.co.uk/2009/12/17/russian_data_cherrypicked_says_sceptic/

3. "Was Russian Climate Data Tampered With?," AccuWeather, December 18, 2009

4. Richard S. Lindzen, "Climate Science: Is it currently designed to answer questions?," November 29, 2008

5. Ibid

6. Ibid

7. Robert Downs, "Senior research professors face funding troubles," The Minnesota Daily, September 27, 2009

8. David Almasi, "Economic Stimulus Funds Went to Climategate Scientist," National Center for Public Policy Research, January 14, 2010

9. Boise State University, http://news.boisestate.edu/blog/2009/11/first-quarter-total-for-external-research-and-grant-awards/

10. University of Wyoming, http://www.uwyo.edu/news/showrelease.asp?id=33943

11. Bret Stephens, "Climategate: Follow the Money," Wall Street Journal, December 1, 2009

12. Ibid

13. Ibid

14. Alastair Jamieson & Louise Gray, "Copenhagen climate summit: deal agreed amid chaos," Telegraph UK, December 19, 2009, http://www.telegraph.co.uk/earth/copenhagen-climate-change-confe/6843304/Copenhagen-climate-summit-deal-agreed-amid-chaos.html

15. David Asman, "On Global Warming: Follow the Money Indeed!," Fox News, February 12, 2007

16. Ibid

17. Steven Milloy, "Al Gore: Climate Pirate," Human Events, November 6, 2009

18. James Kanter, "In London's Financial World, Carbon Trading Is the New Big Thing," New York Times, July 6, 2007

19. Congressional Budget Office, "Trade-Offs in Allocating Allowances for CO2 Emissions," Economic and Budget Issue Brief, April 25, 2007, www.cbo.gov/ftpdocs/80xx/doc8027/04-25-Cap_Trade.pdf.

20. Joshua Rhett Miller, "Fraud in Europe's Cap and Trade System a 'Red Flag,' Critics Say," FoxNews, December 19, 2009

21. Open Europe, "Europe's Dirty Secret: Why the EU Emissions Trading Scheme Isn't Working," August 2007, www.openeurope.org.uk/research/etsp2.pdf.

22. Ibid

23. "Carbon trading susceptible to Enron type frauds," CommodityOnline.com (Courtesy: Businesswire), Febuary 5, 2009, http://www.commodityonline.com/news/Carbon-trading-susceptible-to-Enron-type-frauds-14904-3-1.html

24. Paul J. Georgia, "Enron Sought Global Warming Regulations, Not Free Markets," The Roanoke Times, February 2, 2002

CHAPTER 4: GREEN JOBS, REALLY?

1. Laurent Belsie, "Obama to create 17,000 green jobs. What's a green job?," Christian Science Monitor, January 8, 2010

2. Michael Renner, Sean Sweeney, Jill Kubit, "Green Jobs: Towards decent work in a sustainable, low-carbon world," United Nations Environment Programme (UNEP), September 2008

3. U.S. Department of Labor, "Good Jobs, Safe Jobs, Green Jobs," http://www.dol.gov/dol/green/

4. Mike Carey, Congressional Testimony before the Senate committee on Environment and Public Works

5. Heather Zichal, "Progress on Green Jobs from the Recovery Act," The White House Blog, January 14, 2010

6. "About Us," www.GreenJobs.Com

7. United States Conference of Mayors, "U.S. Metro Economies: Current and Potential Green Jobs In The U.S. Economy," October 2008, http://www.usmayors.org/pressreleases/uploads/GreenJobsReport.pdf

8. Daniel Stone, "What Green Jobs?," Newsweek, July 28, 2009

9. Laurent Belsie, "Obama to create 17,000 green jobs. What's a green job?," Christian Science Monitor, January 8, 2010

10. U.S. Department of Labor, "Good Jobs, Safe Jobs, Green Jobs," http://www.dol.gov/dol/green/

11. "Number Of Green Jobs Could Hit 40 Million By 2030," Environmental Leader, November 9, 2007, http://www.environmentalleader.com/2007/11/09/number-of-green-jobs-could-hit-40-million-by-2030/

12. Andrew P. Morriss, William T. Bogart, Andrew Dorchak, Roger E. Meiners, "Green Jobs Myths," University of Illinois and Case Western Reserve University

13. United States Conference of Mayors, "U.S. Metro Economies: Current and Potential Green Jobs In The U.S. Economy," October 2008, http://www.usmayors.org/pressreleases/uploads/GreenJobsReport.pdf

14. Andrew P. Morriss, William T. Bogart, Andrew Dorchak, Roger F. Meiners, "Green Jobs Myths," University of Illinois and Case Western Reserve University

15. Tony Blankley, "Economic Reality of 5 Million Green Jobs," Rasmussen Reports, May 27, 2009, http://www.rasmussenreports.com/public_content/political_commentary/commentary_by_tony_blankley/economic_reality_of_5_million_green_jobs

16. Gabriel Calzada Alvarez, "Spanish Renewables Bubble," Universidad Rey Juan Carlos, March 2009

17. Ibid

18. Ben Lieberman, "Green Job Subsidies Will Destroy Far More Jobs Than They Create," Heritage Foundation, October 2, 2009

19. Ibid

20. Kay Murchie, "Spain's unemployment rate spirals to 19.3%," Finance Markets, November 3, 2009

21. Ibid

22. US Bureau of Labor Statistic, http://www.bls.gov/bls/unemployment.htm

23. James Parks, "AFL-CIO Announces Center for Green Jobs," AFL-CIO Now Blog, http://blog.aflcio.org

24. Ibid

25. Jenell Walton, "United Steelworkers Union Pushing For Green Jobs", WCPO Ohio, June 23, 2008, http://www.wcpo.com/news/local/story/United-Steelworkers-Union-Pushing-For-Green-Jobs/5ld5qHfPhEqQUnxlcc27WQ.cspx

26. BlueGreen Alliance, About Us Webpage, http://www.bluegreenalliance.org/about_us

27. US Bureau of Labor Statistic, "Union Members Summary 2008", http://www.bls.gov/news.release/union2.nr0.htm

28. Ibid

29. U.S.Department of Labor, (January 6, 2010) "U.S.Department of Labor announces $100 million in green jobs training grants through Recovery Act", Press Release

30. Ibid

31. Ibid

CHAPTER 5: FIRE AND ICE, REALLY?

This was reprinted with permission from the authors and the Business & Media Institute and division of the Media Research Center therefore, reference are formated per said copyright.

Newspapers

1. Associated Press Worldstream 2006 January 29, 2006 Bill Clinton: Climate change is the world's biggest worry

2. Atlanta Constitution July 21, 1923 Radio Ship May find Large Coal Fields in Arctic

3. Boston Daily Globe May 28, 1923 Research Aim Of Arctic Trip

4. Canadian Press Newswire April 4, 2004 Polar Bears Stalk Streets Of Arctic Hamlets; Hunters Seek Higher Kill Quota

5. Chicago Daily Tribune November 6, 1939 Experts Puzzle Over 20 Year Mercury Rise

6. Chicago Tribune August 16, 1998 Editorial Page

7. Christian Science Monitor July 3, 1923 Captain MacMillan Ready to Cast Off For Arctic Cruise

8. Christian Science Monitor August 27, 1974 Major Crop Failures Foreseen

9. Chicago Daily Tribune August 9, 1923 Scientist Says Arctic Ice Will Wipe

Out Canada

10. Columbus Dispatch December 16, 2004 Warming May Send Songbirds North; As Climate Changes, Animals Are Forced To Move, Report Says

11. Edmonton Journal December 29, 2004 Polar Bears Defy Extinction Warnings: Their Numbers are Growing In Nunavut, A Risk To Residents and a Boon to Hunters

12. Evening News (Edinburgh) December 2, 2002 Wonder Machine to Take World by Storm

13. The Independent January 29, 1998 Weather: Spotting a Change in Climate

14. The Independent September 15, 2004 The Global Warming Crisis: These Small Steps on Climate Change Fall Short of the Drastic Solutions We Need

15. Los Angeles Times May 23, 1902 Disappearing Glaciers

16. Los Angeles Times October 7, 1932 Fifth Ice Age Is On The Way

17. Los Angeles Times June 28, 1923 Ice-Age Theory will be Sifted

18. Los Angeles Times April 6, 1924 New Ice-Age is Forecast

19. Los Angeles Times March 11, 1929 Is Another Ice Age Coming?

20. Los Angeles Times December 16, 2005 2005 Vying With '98 as Record Hot Year

21. Los Angeles Times January 9, 2006 Polar Bears Face New Toxic Threat: Flame Retardants

22. New York Times February 24, 1867 The Glacial Period

23. New York Times February 24, 1895 Prospects of Another Glacial Period

24. New York Times October 7, 1912 Sees Glacial Era Coming

25. New York Times September 20, 1922 Penguin Startles France

26. New York Times June 10, 1923 Menace of a New Ice Age to be Tested by Scientists

27. New York Times June 24, 1923 MacMillan Sails on Trip to Arctic

28. New York Times July 4, 1923 MacMillan Sails North

29. New York Times September 28, 1924 MacMillan Reports Signs of New Ice Age

30. The New York Times May 15, 1932 Next Great Deluge Forecast by Science

31. New York Times March 27, 1933 America in Longest Warm Spell Since 1776; Temperature Line Records a 25-Year Rise

32. New York Times August 10, 1952 Our Changing Climate

33. New York Times July 12, 1953 The Weather is Really Changing

34. New York Times February 15, 1959 A Warmer Earth Evident at Poles

35. New York Times February 20, 1969 Expert Says Arctic Ocean Will Soon Be an Open Sea

36. New York Times January 27, 1972 Climate Experts Assay Ice Age Clues

37. New York Times August 8, 1974 Climate Changes Endanger World's Food Output

38. New York Times December 29, 1974 Forecast for Forecasting: Cloudy

39. New York Times January 19, 1975 Climate Changes Called Ominous

40. New York Times May 21, 1975 Scientists Ask Why World Climate Is Changing; Major Cooling May Be Ahead.

41. New York Times August 22, 1981 News Summary

42. New York Times August 13, 1991 Ranges Of Animals and Plants Head North

43. New York Times April 16, 1993 TV Weekend; World Ends Not With a Bang, but a Heat Wave

44. New York Times December 8, 2002 Arctic Ice Is Melting at Record Level, Scientists Say

45. New York Times January 2, 2005 The Future of Calamity

46. New York Times May 20, 2005 Warming Is Blamed for Antarctica's Weight Gain

47. New York Times September 14, 2005 Using Central Park to Study Global

Warming and Flooding

48. New York Times September 27, 2005 'Fire Bell' In the Night

49. New York Times October 25, 2005 No Escape: Thaw Gains Momentum

50. New York Times December 27, 2005 Past Hot Times Hold Few Reasons to Relax About New Warming

51. New York Times December 30, 2005 While You Were Sleeping

52. The Scotsman January 27, 2006 Nightmare Vision of a World 200 Years On

53. Telegraph February 2, 2006 We've Lost Our Fear of Hellfire, But Put Climate Change in its Place

54. Washington Post August 10, 1923 Volcanoes in Australia; Ice Age Coming Here

55. Washington Post October 28, 1928 An Ice – Free World, What Then?

56. Washington Post August 2, 1930 Hot Weather

57. Washington Post May 3, 1932 Second World Flood Seen, if Earth's Heat Increases

58. Washington Post January 11, 1970 Colder Winters Held Dawn of New Ice Age

59. Washington Post January 18, 2006 Is It Warm in Here?; We Could Be Ignoring the Biggest Story in Our History

60. Washington Post March 8, 2006 The Planet Can't Wait

Magazines

61. Atlantic December 1932 This Cold, Cold World

62. Discover Oct. 1989

63. Fortune August 1954 Climate – the Heat May Be Off

64. Fortune February 1974 Ominous Changes in the World's Weather

65. Fortune 2004 February 9, 2004 The Pentagon's Weather Nightmare; The Climate Could Change Radically, and Fast. That Would Be The Mother Of

All National Security Issues

66. International Wildlife July-August 1975 In the Grip of a New Ice Age?

67. National Geographic November 1976 What's Happening to Our Climate?

68. Newsweek April 28, 1975 The Cooling World

69. Newsweek May 20, 1991 On the Wings of Icarus

70. Newsweek (Atlantic Edition) June 30, 2003 Sky High

71. Newsweek August 8, 2005 A European Sahara?

72. Science News Nov 15, 1969 Earth's Cooling Climate

73. Science News March 1, 1975 Climate Change: Chilling Possibilities

74. Science News January 22, 2000 As Globe Warms, Atmosphere Keeps Its Cool

75. Time September 10, 1923 MacMillan Heard From

76. Time January 2, 1939 Warmer World

77. Time October 29, 1951 Retreat of the Cold

78. Time June 24, 1974 Another Ice Age?

79. Time November 11, 1974 Weather Change: Poorer Harvets

80. Time November 13, 2000 Stormy Weather; Are Europe's Floods, Gales and Droughts Here to Stay? Yes, Say the Experts--and it Could Get Worse

81. Time 2001 April 9, 2001 Life In The Greenhouse

82. U.S. News & World Report January 8, 1954 Are Winters Getting Warmer?

83. U.S. News & World Report May 31, 1976 Worrisome CIA Report; Even U.S. Farms May be Hit by Cooling Trend

84. U.S. News & World Report 1993 February 8, 1993 Feeding a World of 10 Billion

85. U.S. News & World Report 1998 May 4, 1998 Just How Hot is it Going to Get?

86. U.S. News & World Report February 11, 2005 Turning Up the Heat; New studies Show that the Earth is Warming up Faster than we Thought. What Can be Done?

Scientific Journals

87. J. B. Kincer September 1933 Monthly Weather Review

88. G. S. Callendar 1938 Quarterly Journal of the Royal Meteorological Society

89. Jonathan A. Patz et al. 17 November 2005 Nature 438, 310-317

Books

90. Ponte, Lowell 1976 The Cooling

91. Baxter, William J. 1953 Today's Revolution in Weather!

92. Gore, Al 1992 Earth in the Balance

93. Schneider, Stephen 1976 The Genesis Strategy

Internet

94. Failing ocean current raises fears of mini ice age, http://www.newscientist.com/article/dn8398

95. For global cooling, just spray, http://www.newscientist.com/article/dn8162

96. What's Going On With the Arctic? (Heartland)

97. The Public and Climate Change (American Institute of Physics), http://www.aip.org/history/climate/Public.htm

98. Global Warming?

99. Prophets of Doom, http://97.74.65.51/readArticle.aspx?ARTID=23124

100. What To Do about Greenhouse Warming: Look Before You Leap

101. Malthusian Warming, http://www.tcsdaily.com/article.aspx?id=032305H

102. Settling Global Warming Science, http://www.tcsdaily.com/article.aspx?id=081204D

103. 20th Century Climate Not So Hot, http://www.cfa.harvard.edu/news/archive/pr0310.html

CHAPTER 6: HERETICS, REALLY?

1. Heretic. (2010). *"Merriam-Webster Online Dictionary."* Retrieved January 27, 2010, from http://www.merriam-webster.com/dictionary/heretic

2. Michael Barone, "How climate-change fanatics corrupted science," The Washington Examiner, February 3, 2010

3. Marc Morano, "Update: 'Consensus' Takes Another Hit! More than 60 German Scientists Dissent Over Global Warming Claims! Call Climate Fears 'Pseudo 'Religion'; Urge Chancellor to 'reconsider' views," Climate Depot, August 04, 2009

4. Guy Dauncey, "The Climate Challenge," New Society Publishers, 2009

5. David Wallechinsky, "The World's 10 Worst Dictators," March 22, 2009

6. Mariano Castillo, "U.S. report Chavez moving to silence media critics," CNN, August 18, 2009

7. David Wallechinsky, "The World's 10 Worst Dictators," March 22, 2009

8. Richard Lindzen, "Climate of Fear Global-warming alarmists intimidate dissenting scientists into silence" Global Research, April 12, 2006

9. Ibid

10. Ibid

11. Fox News, "U.N. Climate Chief: Critics Should Rub Their Faces with Asbestos," Feburary 5, 2010, http://www.foxnews.com/scitech/2010/02/05/climate-chief-critics-rub-faces-asbestos/?test=latestnews

12. Ellen Goodman, "No Change in Political Climate," The Boston Globe, February 8, 2007, http://www.boston.com/news/globe/editorial_opinion/oped/articles/2007/02/09/no_change_in_political_climate/

13. Marc Morano, "Weather Channel Climate Expert Calls for Decertifying Global Warming Skeptics," January 17, 2007, http://epw.senate.gov/public/index.cfm?FuseAction=PressRoom.Blogs&ContentRecord_id=32abc0b0-802a-23ad-440a-88824bb8e528

14. Ibid

15. Rich Noyes, "The Left's Climategate: A Scandal for Journalism, Too," Media Research Center, December 3, 2009

16. Ibid

17. Ibid

18. Gene J. Koprowski, "U.N.'s Global Warming Report Under Fresh Attack for Rainforest Claims," Foxnews, January 28, 2010

19. Ibid

20. Damian Carrington, "IPCC officials admit mistake over melting Himalayan glaciers," Guardian.co.uk, January 20, 2010, http://www.guardian.co.uk/environment/2010/jan/20/ipcc-himalayan-glaciers-mistake

21. Ibid

22. Ibid

CHAPTER 7: IT HELPS MINORITIES, REALLY?

1. Jane Gross, "After a Ruling, Hawaii Weighs Gay Marriages," New York Times, April 25, 1994

2. Commission to Engage African Americans on Climate Change, "Leaders Kick Off Commission to Engage African Americans on Climate Change," Joint Center for Political and Economic Studies, July 29, 2008

3. National Center for Public Policy Research, "Survey of African-Americans on Energy," June 25, 2009

4. Lea Radick, "Global warming more harmful to low-income minorities," Medill Washington Program, July 24, 2008, and
J. Andrew Hoerner and Nia Robinson, "A Climate of Change: African Americans, Global Warming, and a Just Climate Policy for the U.S.," Environmental Justice and Climate Change Initiative, June 2008

5. Commission to Engage African Americans on Climate Change, "Leaders Kick Off Commission to Engage African Americans on Climate Change," Joint Center for Political and Economic Studies, July 29, 2008

6. Jonathan Leake, "UN wrongly linked global warming to natural disasters," The Sunday Times Online, January 24, 2010

7. Ibid

8. Richard Lindzen, "Climate of Fear Global-warming alarmists intimidate dissenting scientists into silence," Global Research, April 12, 2006

9. Jonathan Leake, "UN wrongly linked global warming to natural disasters," The Sunday Times Online, January 24, 2010

10. Ibid

11. National Oceanic and Atmospheric Administration, "Atlantic Hurricane Climatology and Overview," http://www.ncdc.noaa.gov/oa/climate/research/hurricane-climatology.html

12. Commission to Engage African Americans on Climate Change, "Leaders Kick Off Commission to Engage African Americans on Climate Change," Joint Center for Political and Economic Studies, July 29, 2008

13. J. Andrew Hoerner and Nia Robinson, "A Climate of Change: African Americans, Global Warming, and a Just Climate Policy for the U.S.," Environmental Justice and Climate Change Initiative, June 2008

14. National Center for Public Policy Research, "Survey of African-Americans on Energy," June 25, 2009

15. David Kreutzer, Ph.D., Karen Campbell, Ph.D., William W. Beach, Ben Lieberman, Nicolas Loris, "What Boxer-Kerry will Cost the Economy," Heritage Foundation, January 26, 2010

16. Ibid

17. Ibid

18. V. Doin Haynes, "U.S. unemployment rate for blacks projected to hit 25-year high," Washington Post, January 15, 2010

19. Bureau of Labor Statistics, "Employment status of the civilian population by race, sex, and age," February 3, 2010 from http://www.bls.gov/news. release/empsit.t02.htm

20. Thomas Sowell, "Race, Culture, And Equality,"

CHAPTER 8: SOLUTIONS, REALLY?

1. David Biello, "10 Solutions for Climate Change," Scientific America, November 26, 2007

2. Philip Gallant, "Help to stop using fossil fuels petition," http://www. thepetitionsite.com/1/-help-to-stop-using-fossil-fuels

3. US Energy Information Administration, "Annual Energy Review Report 2008," June 2009, http://tonto.eia.doe.gov/energyexplained/index.cfm

4. David Biello, "10 Solutions for Climate Change," Scientific America, November 26, 2007

5. Ibid

6. Alan Durning, "Air travel heats up the planet," Sightline Institute, August 1, 2004

7. Patrick McGreevy, "State lawmakers seek to end free parking," Los Angeles Times, January 29, 2010

8. David Biello, "10 Solutions for Climate Change," Scientific America, November 26, 2007

9. Guy Dauncey, "The Climate Challenge," New Society Publishers, 2009

10. David Biello, "10 Solutions for Climate Change," Scientific America, November 26, 2007

11. Ibid

12. Environmental Protection Agency, "Greenhouse Gases Threaten Public Health and the Environment / Science overwhelmingly shows greenhouse gas concentrations at unprecedented levels due to human activity,"

December 7, 2009

13. BBC Interview, February 13, 2010, http://news.bbc.co.uk/2/hi/science/ nature/8511670.stm

***

GREGORY E. PARKER

www.ingramcontent.com/pod-product-compliance
Lightning Source LLC
Chambersburg PA
CBHW021832020426
42334CB00014B/590